# BRF

This year we are celebrating t... to Oxford. We are marking th... of ways. In particular we are u... publicize afresh exactly what ... still think of us as simply a p... ently unaware of the 35 books... ministry activity that Anne Hibbert and Sue Doggett are developing, with quiet days and retreats, training days and a host of other events.

## New logo and mission statement

We have adopted a new logo and mission statement. You will see the new logo on the cover of all the May–August notes and on all our new books published since February this year. Created by our designer Louise, it represents the freshness and vitality of BRF in all that we are doing—publishing and ministry. Many people know us as both 'BRF' and 'Bible Reading Fellowship'. We have now moved to using just 'BRF' and so the new logo incorporates both our image and our name.

Our new mission statement is 'Resourcing your Spiritual Journey'. This represents everything that BRF is about, our publications and our ministry activities, which are all designed to help people grow in their relationship with God and their understanding of the Bible and prayer, and so to become more effective disciples of Jesus Christ.

## Improvements to the notes

You will also notice some improvements to the layout of all the Bible reading notes to make them even more accessible and user-friendly.

## Services of celebration and thanksgiving

As advertised in the January 2001 issue, there will be four services of celebration and thanksgiving this year. If you have not already requested tickets to join us for one or more of these occasions, there is still time to do so. You may want to consider bringing a group from your church—we would be delighted to see you! Please use the form overleaf to apply for tickets.

## Retreats and quiet days

We have a programme of over 40 retreats and quiet days for this year! If you haven't yet been on a retreat or quiet day, why not try one with BRF? Several of the days are designed especially for those who haven't experienced this kind of occasion before. All the events provide people with a chance to draw away from their busy lives for a time of teaching, reflection and prayer.

For further details, visit the 'Events' section on the BRF website (www.brf.org.uk) or write to the BRF office for a copy of the full programme.

**Advance information: Pilgrimage to the Holy Land April 2002**

'Once you have been to the Holy Land you'll never read your Bible in the same way again.' This is the testimony of countless pilgrims to Israel—and it is certainly the experience of those who have visited with BRF. During the 1990s Richard Fisher led four BRF pilgrimages to Israel, two of which were jointly led with one of BRF's trustees, Bishop John Went.

A fifth BRF pilgrimage will take place 15–23 April 2002 (which is also BRF's 80th anniversary year!). This will be led by Richard Fisher and Revd Graham Usher, who is a BRF trustee and vicar of an inner-city parish in Middlesbrough. He is an experienced pilgrimage leader who has also worked in Jerusalem.

For further information and booking details please send an A4 27p s.a.e., clearly marked 'Pilgrimage' in the top left-hand corner, to the BRF office in Oxford. All information will also be available on the BRF website.

---

(PLEASE PRINT)

Name: _____

Address: _____

_____ Postcode: _____

Tel. (day): _____ (evening): _____

**Please send me tickets for the following service(s):**

| | Qty |
|---|---|
| ☐ Saturday 12 May 2001, St Helen's Parish Church, 2.00pm | _____ |
| ☐ Saturday 9 June 2001, Christchurch, Clifton, Bristol, 2.00pm | _____ |
| ☐ Saturday 22 Sept 2001, Durham Cathedral, 2.00pm | _____ |
| ☐ Saturday 27 Oct 2001, Bury St Edmunds Cathedral, 2.00pm | _____ |

**Total number of tickets:** _____

**Please send your completed form to:** 2001 Service Ticket Dept, BRF, Peter's Way, Sandy Lane West, Oxford OX4 6HG

Ticket applications will be processed strictly on a first-come, first-served basis. We will advise you if your application arrives after all the tickets have been allocated. If you do not hear from us, you may assume that tickets have been reserved for you as requested, and these will be despatched approximately three weeks before each service takes place.

# DAY BY DAY
# WITH GOD

## Bible Readings for Women

MAY–AUGUST 2001

Christina Press
BRF
Tunbridge Wells/Oxford

BRF, Peter's Way, Sandy Lane West, Oxford, OX4 5HG

First published in Great Britain 2001

ISBN 1 84101 156 8

Jacket design: JAC Design for Print, Crowborough

Trade representation in UK:
Lion Publishing plc, Peter's Way, Sandy Lane West,
Oxford OX4 6HG

Distributed in Australia by:
Willow Connection, PO Box 288, Brookvale, NSW 2100.
Tel: 02 9948 3957; Fax: 02 9948 8153;
E-mail: info@willowconnection.com.au

Distributed in New Zealand by:
Scripture Union Wholesale, PO Box 760, Wellington
Tel: 04 385 0421; Fax: 04 384 3990; E-mail: suwholesale@clear.net.nz

Distributed in South Africa by:
Struik Book Distributors, PO Box 193, Maitland 7405
Tel: 021 551 5900; Fax: 021 551 1124; E-mail: enquiries@struik.co.za

**Acknowledgments**

Scriptures from The New Revised Standard Version of the Bible,
Anglicized Edition, copyright © 1989, 1995 by the Division of
Christian Education of the National Council of the Churches of
Christ in the USA, used by permission. All rights reserved.

Scriptures from The Revised Standard Version of the Bible, copyright
© 1946, 1952, 1971 by the Division of Christian Education of the
National Council of the Churches of Christ in the USA, used by
permission. All rights reserved.

*The Living Bible* copyright © 1971 by Tyndale House Publishers.

Scripture quotations taken from *The Holy Bible, New International
Version*, copyright © 1973, 1978, 1984 by International Bible Society.
Used by permission of Hodder & Stoughton Ltd. All rights reserved.
'NIV' is a registered trademark of International Bible Society. UK
trademark number 1448790.

Scriptures quoted from the Good News Bible published by The Bible
Societies/HarperCollins Publishers Ltd, UK © American Bible Society
1966, 1971, 1976, 1992, used with permission.

Scriptures quoted from The Jerusalem Bible © 1966 by Darton,
Longman & Todd Ltd and Doubleday & Company, Inc.

*The Message* © 1993 by Eugene H. Peterson, NavPress, Colorado
Springs

Printed in Great Britain by Omnia Books Ltd, Glasgow

# Contents

# The Editor writes...

Usually I have no problem with sleeping—but just lately I have been lying awake at night with my mind churning over issues ranging from mundane matters such as 'What do I feed everyone on this weekend?' to much wider issues on the sadnesses and injustices that some people have to endure. The world we live in is far from the perfect place that I am sure God intended it to be, and no amount of fussing and fuming and lying awake at night is going to change that fact.

## Planning

One of the amazing things about editing *Day by Day with God* is the way a main theme seems to come through the notes each issue, even though my initial planning didn't intend it that way! Over the next four months we will be thinking and learning a lot about God's care for us in the dark hours—when everything seems to be not what God would want for us or for our world. Christine Leonard has also been lying awake at night worrying, but she reminds us that God does not go off duty (reading for 3 May), and that if we can only leave the worrying to him he may give us sleep and a new start to each new day.

Paul's first letter to the church in Corinth is amazingly relevant to us as we try to live as Christians in the 21st century (19–31 August). Corinth was a very worldly city and the Christians there did not always manage to be unaffected by the permissive lifestyles of those around them. It is the same today. What is currently considered a 'normal' lifestyle by those around us is not always the way God wants us to live, and it would be much easier and safer to spend all our time with Christian friends. But we are meant to be 'salt' and 'light' in the world (Matthew 5:13–16).

## Lifestyle

It can be quite painful to be 'different' from those around us when there is a clash of lifestyle between what others consider OK and what we know is not OK for a Christian. Our new writer, Fiona Barnard, who has based her notes on Hebrews 11, points out that Noah must have been considered completely odd when he obeyed God and began to build a boat on dry land! She reminds us that when we feel bewildered and fragile, our faith in Christ will be like an anchor and give us hope.

This is why it is important to keep in touch with God. It is only too easy, in our sometimes over-busy lives, to squeeze out the space in our day when we 'key in' to him. I hope that everything that has been written in these notes will give you encouragement and hope and a daily reminder that God is with each one of us—that whatever each day may bring, we are not on our own.

*Mary Reid*

# Contributors

**Beryl Adamsbaum** is a language teacher living in France, just across the border from Geneva, Switzerland, where she and her husband have been engaged in Christian ministry for thirty years. She is involved in teaching, preaching and counselling. She is the editor of her church magazine and writes short devotional articles.

**Diana Archer** has three young children and a degree in religious studies, and has served in Japan as a missionary. She has worked in the publishing world as a freelance editor and writer. Her book *Who'd Plant a Church?* (Christina Press) has been highly acclaimed.

**Fiona Barnard** lives in Scotland. Her principal work is among international students, encouraging local churches to reach out in friendship to those temporarily far from home.

**Celia Bowring** is the compiler of CARE's *Prayer Guide*, which highlights family and community issues and political and ethical concerns. Her recent book *The Special Years* is for parents of children under five. She works closely with her husband, Lyndon, in CARE, and is a contributor to several periodicals.

**Anne Coomes** has been a journalist for the Church of England for nearly twenty years. Together with the well-known artist Taffy Davies, she has launched www.parishpump.co.uk, a website providing articles for parish magazine editors. Anne also does freelance communications work for various dioceses, and has written five books. She holds a degree in theology and is Reader for her parish in north Cheshire.

**Jennifer Rees Larcombe** is one of Britain's best-loved Christian authors and speakers. She has written many books, and her latest—*Beauty from Ashes* (BRF, 2000)—is to help those suffering from grief, loss or trauma. As well as speaking at many conferences, she also leads retreats and quiet days at her home in Kent.

**Christine Leonard** lives in Surrey with her husband and two teenage children. She writes books for both adults and children; most tell the true stories of ordinary Christians who have done extraordinary things. She is the Vice President of the Association of Christian Writers and the author of *Affirming Love* (BRF, 1999).

**Wendy Pritchard** is the wife of John, Archdeacon of Canterbury. She is an enthusiastic part-time maths teacher, and mother to two daughters in their early twenties. Wendy has enjoyed each different phase of her life, from vicar's wife to mass caterer, and is interested in gardening, computing and solving life's problems.

**Christina Rees** was born in America and came to live in England twenty years ago when she met and married Chris Rees. She is a freelance writer and broadcaster, speaker, preacher and a member of the General Synod of the Church of England and the Archbishops' Council. She is also Chair of WATCH (Women and the Church), a national organization that provides a forum for promoting women in the Church.

**Alie Stibbe** has contributed to *Renewal* and other Christian publications. She lives at St Andrew's Vicarage, Chorleywood, where her husband Mark is the vicar. Previously they ministered in Sheffield and have four children.

**Contributors are identified by their initials
at the bottom of each page.**

# A Morning Prayer

*Thank you, heavenly Father,*
*for this new day.*
*Be with me now*
*in all I do*
*and think*
*and say,*
*that it will be to your glory.*

*Amen*

# Only the bright hours?

*The heavens are telling the glory of God; and the firmament proclaims his handiwork. Day to day pours forth speech and night to night declares knowledge.*

'I record only the bright hours.' When I saw this sentence engraved on a sun-dial it struck me not only as smug but ridiculous. Since when did a sun-dial *record* anything? Anyway, given the British climate, who needs such a fair-weather friend?

I'm so grateful that God does not record only our bright hours, when we're doing well and feeling full of praise, but I have to keep holding on to that truth. It's all too easy to veer towards the lie that God loves us only when we have it all together. Often in church or talking with Christians I get the impression that if anything goes wrong it must be of the devil—and if I feel down or gloomy in any way it must be my sin. Not necessarily! Over these twelve days we'll be exploring God and our relationship with him, not in the sunny hours but in the dark and the night.

Of course we all know 'God is light and in him is no darkness at all' (1 John 1:5), yet the Bible does often show him owning dark places too. 'Yours is the day, yours also the night' insists Psalm 74:16 while Isaiah 45:7 states, 'I form light and create darkness'. In Psalm 19 God 'declares knowledge' through the night.

In practice it's often the dark, difficult, stormy times when he takes a special interest in us. Even though we don't always recognize him in the stress of the moment, that's when we grow and when he uses us most to help others. We shouldn't be surprised. Over and over again the Bible tells us how he speaks to people during dark times, changing their lives.

---

*I'm so grateful that you are Lord of both day and night and that your love and grace shine right inside the darkest places.*

**CL**

# Day and night, night and day

*The Lord went in front of them in a pillar of cloud by day, to lead them along the way, and in a pillar of fire by night, to give them light, so that they might travel by day and by night.*

At midnight, passing over the Israelite slaves, the Lord caused unendurable grief to the despot Egyptians. At long last, they let his people go. Here the Israelites are camping on the edge of the wilderness, the Red Sea still ahead of them. God avoided leading them by the direct route through the land of the Philistines lest, facing war, they 'change their minds and return to Egypt'. Free (though not yet guaranteed long-term freedom) after generations of slavery, the demoralized Israelites have little idea of the way forward. Disorientated, like hostages standing blinking on the steps of a plane after years in blindfolded captivity, they need specialised help to guide them away from this country of terrors.

When I don't know which way to turn, I long for pillars of cloud and fire, or at least for some writing in the sky to spell out the best course of action—but perhaps it's enough to know that, in extreme situations, God can provide. And how! The amazing sign of his presence even allowed his people to travel by night—a pillar of fire proving more effective than any braziers or oil-lamps the most powerful Egyptians could muster. Night-vision always was a strategic tool. After the years when God appeared to have abandoned them, his people, no longer limited by darkness, find comfort in that, 'neither the pillar of cloud by day nor the pillar of fire by night left its place in front of (them)'.

---

*Father God, be with your people who suffer extremes and night-terrors, giving comfort and vision. And when the darkness seems to press in around and we don't know where to turn, may all of us sense your presence as strongly as those Israelites did in their wilderness.*

**CL**

# Strike in the night

*He will not let your foot be moved; he who keeps you will not slumber. He who keeps Israel will neither slumber nor sleep. The Lord is your keeper; the Lord is your shade at your right hand. The sun shall not strike you by day nor the moon by night.*

At three in the morning, there's nothing to distract us from pain or worry. We can't disturb other people's sleep just to find some much-needed comfort, so everything seems mega-bleak and dreadful. But God never goes off duty. If—and it's a big if—we can only trust, relax and leave the worrying to him he may give us sleep, and a new start for a new day. Then, when noon approaches and the heat's on, he'll be our 'shade'.

That probably sounds glib—yet for many in the world the truth contained in this Psalm is anything but easy. Whenever I read it I think of Ugandan Christians in Kampala during the dark terrors of Amin's years. They too would lift up their eyes to the hills, where many of their number had fled. Yet their help had ultimately to be, not in the hills, but in the Lord. The Psalm says that he will 'keep your life'. Many of those Christians, including their Archbishop, Janani Luwum, lost theirs. Had God deserted them? Was he asleep? Had the brute strength of the darkness defeated him and his people? No, they emerged from that time with churches much stronger and more vibrant than before. What about us? Would we dare stay with him through the night, as they did?

---

*Lord, help us to learn what it is to live in your shadow and shelter so that, even if we find ourselves in times of great trial we may not fear 'the terror of the night, or the arrow that flies by day, or the pestilence that stalks in darkness, or the destruction that wastes at noonday'.*

*Read Psalm 91.*

CL

# Praying by night

*I think of you on my bed and meditate on you in the watches of the night; for you have been my help, and in the shadow of your wings I sing for joy.*

'Now, you know it's really important to start each day with prayer and Bible reading!' Maybe—but in researching these notes I've been struck by the number of times the Bible talks about praying at night. It's a bit of a relief because some of my best praying is done at night when the phone doesn't ring and I'm not thinking, 'Crumbs, I'd better take that meat out of the freezer before I forget again!' If I find myself unable to sleep and do manage to pray it can be a very special time.

I love that image of singing for joy under the shadow of his wings. Psalm 42:8 has God joining in—or is it we who join with him? 'By day the Lord commands his steadfast love, and at night his song is with me, a prayer to the God of my life.' That's from a man whose soul is cast down!

In Israel the priests ministered, prayed and worshipped day and night in the temple. Anna, an 84-year-old widow, never left it but 'worshipped there with fasting and praying night and day' (Luke 2:37). We too are asked to 'pray without ceasing' and sometimes, having done everything, simply to 'stand firm', as Ephesians 6:13 says. Like the priests who 'stand by night' and bless God in Psalm 134, all we may be able to do is to lift our hands and hearts to the holy place—and that's enough. (Of course consideration for others may mean that at night we have to 'stand' lying down, just as we sing silently.)

---

*Lord, I admire monks and nuns who rise every night to worship in cold chapels, but I am grateful that we can worship you even in bed, for you look on the heart and have made our bodies temples of the Holy Spirit.*

**CL**

# Wakey, wakey!

*I bless the Lord who gives me counsel; in the night also
my heart instructs me.*

The Bible's words about noctur-
nal communication cover more
than our prayers and worship.
God makes a habit of speaking
to people in the middle of the
night. After a quick scan
through the concordance I
found that the Bible takes the
trouble to mention that God
spoke at night-time to Abime-
lech, Abraham, Laban the
Aramean, Balaam, Gideon,
Samuel, Nathan, Solomon,
Zechariah, and Jesus (in that he
prayed all night before choosing
his disciples). God spoke to such
diverse characters as Jacob/
Israel and Saul/Paul so often in
the night that I found myself
wondering, flippantly, if they
suffered from sleep deprivation.
All that highly charged communication certainly did something. Each changed not only
his name but his nature.

Interesting, isn't it? Some of
the people in my list were good
and some of them weren't: some
worshipped God and some did
not. Some are well known and
some, you're probably thinking
'Who?!' Some were given com-
missions, or encouragement,
warned of danger or given strate-
gies, others were told off in no
uncertain terms. Some received
dreams or visions, others words.

Why does God speak by
night? Who knows in the case of
all these amazing people? All I
know is that there's absolutely
no point in my grumbling if God
thumps me awake at two in the
morning. It's my own fault for
not listening to him at a more
convenient hour. There's no
point either in trying to drop off
to sleep again until I've paid him
some serious attention. But isn't
it as well that he doesn't operate
'only in the bright hours'?

---

*God, you are God. You don't
march to our time scales; you
speak in surprising ways to surprising people and you say surprising things. Help us not to be
absurd in trying to mould you to
our own image. Instead keep us
attentive to listen to you and
learn your ways.*

**CL**

15

# Jacob 1

*He came to a certain place and stayed there for the night, because the sun had set. Taking one of the stones of the place, he put it under his head and lay down in that place... and dreamed... and the Lord said, '...the land on which you lie I will give to you and to your offspring.'*

Quiet mother's boy Jacob enjoyed home-life and cooking. Having cheated his older twin, Esau, out of his blessing and inheritance, how hard it must have been to flee from his family, from all he had known and journey through the wilderness towards an uncle he had never met! Alone in the darkness that first night he'd no idea where he was and could find only a stone for a pillow. Yet that was when God chose to open heaven to him, revealing angels ascending and descending, then giving him, in person, great promises— of this land (which Jacob was leaving), of a vast family who would bless all the families of earth (though Jacob had never been more alone) and of his own abiding presence and protection (though Jacob was bound for a land where people worshipped other gods).

God still speaks to people in the darkest, loneliest times, as he did to Jacob. His ways are not our ways. The times when we feel we deserve nothing but punishment from him are the very times when he pronounces extravagant blessing. Our time-scales are not his time-scales. Often the more definite the promise the longer the wait. Jacob had to hold on very tight to his promises through years of long days and nights in which the cheater was cheated by his wily Uncle Laban.

---

*What promises has God made to you, by night or day? Which have you seen fulfilled and which have almost disappeared from your sight? Try to appropriate verse 15 to yourself today: 'Know that I am with you and will keep you wherever you go, and will bring you back to this (promise); for I will not leave you until I have done what I promised you.'*

**CL**

16

# Jacob 2

*The same night he got up and took his two wives, his two maids
and his eleven children, and crossed the ford of the Jabbok…
left alone… a man wrestled with him until daybreak…
and blessed him.*

Finally Jacob, with a great company of his wives, children and flocks, arrives back on the borders of his promised land, but he has a big problem. Nothing's been resolved with Esau, the brother he cheated. On home territory Esau has every right, plus the power, to kill them all. Do read Jacob's prayer (vv. 9–12). He's gained hugely in humility and even gained a certain authority from trusting in God, yet come nightfall, at the crossing of the 'Rubicon' border river, he's so afraid he doesn't know where he is.

Once again he's alone, in the darkness… and yet he isn't. A man appears and wrestles with him until daybreak. Not until afterwards does Jacob identify the mysterious stranger as God—and is astounded to have seen God face to face yet survived. What an extraordinary story—and yet aren't there times when we have all struggled with something, through long night hours, only to realize that it was God rather than ourself, our enemy or our fear?

This time God himself blesses Jacob, renaming him Israel, because he has 'striven with God and with humans and has prevailed.' Now the 'big problem' is resolved easily. Esau meets his brother in a spirit of forgiveness and generosity, while Jacob does everything to make amends. Walking with a limp, with a new name, a new identity and a new inheritance, Jacob can begin the rest of his life.

---

*May we meet you when we're on
the borders, way beyond where
we feel we can cope. May we
find and wrestle with you in the
darkness there Lord, rather than
be defeated by our fear or guilt or
despair. May we find we change
and may we find you faithful.*

**CL**

# Jacob 3

*God spoke to Israel in visions of the night, and said, 'Jacob, Jacob... do not be afraid to go down to Egypt, for I will make of you a great nation there. I myself will go down with you to Egypt, and I will bring you up again; and Joseph's own hand shall close your eyes.'*

For all the blessings and promises Jacob had received from God, he still made plenty of errors. Favouring his son Joseph above his other sons led to terrible betrayal and grief—then, in his old age, famine struck the promised land. On a much less cosmic scale, I shouted at my daughter last Sunday. She was kindly helping me make lunch after I'd rushed back from church, but just when we were dishing up and everything needed doing at once she spilled orange juice all over herself and the floor. My stress and her hurt marred what should have been a bright hour. After I apologized and we hugged, brightness returned, but I need to seek God about my reactions because this wasn't a one-off.

Repeating Jacob's old name (not 'Israel') God spoke again in the night. Why continue to give blessings and promises to someone as mixed up as Jacob, whose life-changes proved so fickle? All I know is that it gives us hope. Even when we receive God's promises and blessing and then mess up completely, he will re-draw the plan, even making it bigger. It may prove complicated, we may have some painful lessons to learn—but he'll restore his purposes in the end—bringing light and his own rule and reign even into the darkness of an Egypt. Meanwhile he won't stop caring for and speaking with us.

---

*Thank you God that you're not interested only in our bright hours. A redeemer not only of individuals, your goodness affects whole countries and societies, like the prison population in Argentina and gypsy peoples right across Europe. May we seek your visions and presence in the night, that we might take our part in your purposes on earth.*

CL

# Black's white

*Ah, you who call evil good and good evil, who put darkness for light and light for darkness, who put bitter for sweet and sweet for bitter! Ah, you who are wise in your own eyes, and shrewd in your own sight.*

'I always say the main thing is, you've got to be true to yourself. You've fallen for that hunk in the office, he treats you better than Dave ever did. No point thinking about the children—your unhappiness isn't going to make them happy. You're concerned about young Sam, drinking till he makes himself sick every weekend? He's fifteen, Sharon, and if he enjoys it…! You don't understand how he can enjoy it? That's the trouble with you, Sharon, no tolerance. He's not driving a car so he's not doing anyone any harm. It's not on, you know, stopping other people being themselves!

'Thing is, Sharon, you've never learnt to look out for number one. Be self-sufficient, like the Government's always telling us. Best move I made—when I left Nick. Who needs men when you can live by yourself and do your own thing? Can't be wrong when 80% of new houses are bought by 'loners' like me. Waste of resources? Really, Sharon, you're so old fashioned! Anyway Ruff lives here too, though he's not getting any younger, poor doggie, and the vet's bills are something shocking.

'What's that? This isn't a social visit? You're collecting on behalf of "Save the Children"? No, I don't want to see pictures of half-starved kids. Anyway they're not my problem. Only sad people give to charity, Sharon. Get a life!'

---

*Lord, I'm no better than 'Sharon's friend'. You say it's good to trust you, to be poor, meek, to mourn and hunger, to be merciful and pure, to make peace and be persecuted. I live as though it's best to worry. I chase financial security, my rights and happiness. I gossip sometimes and shout at people. But in putting myself first I'm walking in darkness and losing my life. Help, Lord!*

CL

19

# A dark God?

*Then the people stood at a distance, while Moses drew near to the thick darkness where God was.*

God has just given his people the ten commandments, in order that they will be holy as he is holy—so what is he doing in the 'thick darkness' of this frightening passage, with thunder and lightning, trumpet blasts, mountains smoking and the people begging Moses not to let God speak to them lest they die? Has God turned into some kind of villain? No, Moses explains, 'God has come only to test you and to put the fear of him upon you so that you do not sin.' The 'darkness where God was' had to do with his holiness, not sin. Were the Victorians right then, believing in a dark, vengeful deity? Should we too write 'Thou God seest me' at the foot of our beds? No, the fear motive has always proved ineffective in preventing humans from rebelling. Even the Israelites who witnessed this dark terror were soon breaking the commandments and making another god to worship.

Sin is indeed terrible and God longs to save us from it but, since Jesus died the death that we all deserve, he has found a better way. Now we come not to a 'blazing fire and darkness and gloom and a tempest' as Hebrews 12:18 says. Instead, through Jesus' sacrifice, we have come to 'Mount Zion and to the city of the living God, the heavenly Jerusalem, and to innumerable angels in festal gathering' (Hebrews 12:22). Praise God it is his grace, not law and punishment, which leads to repentance and lavish, extraordinary new beginnings.

---

*Lord, help us to walk out of darkness as we're drawn by your light and love. Read Hebrews 12:18–24 and consider God in his holiness not as dark, impenetrable, terrifying but as a wonderful light that you can approach. Clothed in the white robe which Jesus holds out to you, feel at home as you draw near in full assurance of faith, to rest in his presence and absorb his holy ways.*

CL

# Dark-light

*From noon on, darkness came over the whole land until three in the afternoon. And about three o'clock Jesus cried with a loud voice… 'My God, my God, why have you forsaken me?'*

God's grace offers us salvation from the darkness of sin, but it is not cheap grace. The price he paid meant involving his very self in the darkness. That's astounding enough at the Incarnation. John 1:5 says, 'The light shines in the darkness and the darkness did not overcome it.' At Golgotha the darkness did appear to overcome. As the unthinkable happened and our sin caused God to be separated from God, no wonder darkness fell across the earth at noonday.

I have in front of me a re-production of Salvador Dali's famous painting of the crucifix-ion. We view Jesus as God the Father might. His crucified body, suspended above the world, reflects down on it the light of heaven and holds back the vast darkness of space. Somehow Jesus is immensely strong (the composition, the muscles) yet weak and dying; he's fully human yet fully divine. Only crucifixion could have produced the extraordinary shape of his foreshortened body, bent neck and outstretched arms. Here is death but also new life.

Dali painted this picture in 1951, in response to Hiroshima —an amazing statement of God's attitude in the face of the continuing dark suffering of humanity and of the planet which he made. The earth below the cross is not a Galilean lake and boat as I'd always sup-posed, nor is it Hiroshima, but a Spanish fishing port near Dali's home. He's declaring the truth that the pivotal moment of the crucifixion happened not only in time and space, but every-where and always. When Light took on itself the darkness, the Light did, and will, overcome.

---

*Thank Jesus who took upon him-self darkness, so we can know light—for he continues to hold back the darkness and reflect God's light to us, until darkness shall be no more.*

CL

# Christians—lights in the night?

**We know that this is truly the Saviour of the world.**

Jesus attempted to shed some light when Nicodemus came to him by night. The woman at the well met him at noonday but she was just as much in the dark, an outcast with men-problems. She came from a Samaritan town which had strayed from the faith of their forefather Jacob. They'd kept his well but lost the right idea about worshipping God. Jesus' light exposed some uncomfortable truths but nevertheless freed the woman to worship God in spirit and in truth and also to form clean relationships. She went and told the rest of the town, Jesus lit up their lives too and the defiled place became holy again.

In order to enter other people's nights and rescue them Jesus broke all the taboos—speaking to a woman on her own (especially *that* kind of woman!), Jew speaking to despised Samaritan, man asking woman for help, rabbi giving spiritual instruction to a lone female… Most of us Christians in Britain are much more respectable. We don't go out to nightclubs or New Age gatherings or sit in subways with homeless people; we don't visit prisons or engage fat-cat bosses in deep conversations; we keep our distance from racists, drug dealers, traffic wardens and slimy politicians. We're too busy in church meetings to speak out against injustice. We switch our lights on when we're together on Sundays and off afterwards, lest the darkness outside overcome them. And so those in darkness never see the light.

---

*Jesus, we claim to follow you of whom it was said 'the people who walked in darkness have seen a great light; those who lived in a land of deep darkness—on them light has shined'. You were never there only for the bright hours and the holy people. Show us today where you want each of us to focus the particular beam of light which you have given us— and help us to trust you as you trust us to shine.*

**CL**

# Don't put burdens on others

*And God, who knows the human heart, testified to them by giving them the Holy Spirit, just as he did to us; and in cleansing their hearts by faith he has made no distinction between them and us.*

At least ten years have passed since Peter met with Cornelius in Caesarea. As a result of that meeting, Cornelius, who was a Gentile, and all his household, as well as others listening, became filled with the Holy Spirit and were baptized by Peter. After that, the good news of Jesus Christ was also preached to the Gentiles wherever the disciples went.

In the intervening time, some of the Jewish Christians began to say that salvation was gained by faith and circumcision. They wanted to require that male Gentile converts also be circumcised. Finally, the apostles and elders met together in what is called the Council at Jerusalem. After much debate Peter addressed the assembly and argued that grace alone was sufficient for salvation. He challenged the gathering by accusing them of placing a yoke around the necks of the Gentiles that God had never intended. In the end, Peter won the argument about circumcision, but agreed with those who insisted on a few basic purity laws—as long as they weren't seen as a means of salvation.

How often do we attempt to add 'extras' to the message that salvation is by God's grace alone? What are we communicating to those outside the faith about their role in their own salvation? Do *you* believe that you have been saved by God's grace—or by something else?

---

*Dear Lord, let me remember that my new life in Christ is a gift from you. No matter how good I am, I can never earn salvation: no matter how bad I am, you will never withdraw your love from me. Amen.*

**CR**

# The bare essentials

*For it has seemed good to the Holy Spirit and to us to impose on you no further burden than these essentials: that you abstain from what has been sacrificed to idols and from blood and from what is strangled and from fornication. If you keep yourself from these you will do well.*

In yesterday's reading, Peter stressed the conviction that salvation is through faith in Jesus and is a gift of God's grace. Today, we focus on what Peter, Paul and the other disciples felt were the minimum requirements for Gentile converts to live a godly life.

Their list of the bare essentials seems rather strange to us in a faith culture that no longer includes stringent purity laws. Every item on the short list of taboos would have been involved in some way in sacrilegious worship, hence its prohibition.

Based on the criteria for the disciples' list, an equivalent list for us today might forbid the taking part in occult practices or worship, or in any ceremonies that exalted a false god. Even the disciples' inclusion of fornication in this instance had to do with legal impurity, and not with sexual morality.

Of course, the disciples would have gone on to teach the former heathens how to live more fully as Christians, but, initially, there were only a few things that were strictly forbidden.

---

*Dear Lord, please show us how to live so that we bring you joy and build up the body of Christ. Help us to welcome new Christians with the same graciousness with which you have welcomed us. Amen.*

**CR**

# Who is strengthening you?

*Judas and Silas, who were themselves prophets, said much to encourage and strengthen the believers.*

In any individual Christian's life of faith there has to be a balance between giving out and taking in. By far the most common imbalance I see in my friends is that they are continually giving out, and they pay scant heed to taking in and being fed by others.

It is possible to live a life of imbalance for a while, but sooner or later, something will give. You, or one of your family, will get ill or work will pile up or something will happen to make you realize that, once again, you've been living a lopsided life.

I expect it happens to most people, and possibly the only way to guard against it for certain is to become a recluse! However, most of us can do better, and need to, if we are to live effective and healthy lives, and retain our sense of joy. Perhaps a quick checklist reveals an imbalance. When was the last time you prayed with other Christians? Is there something you are bottling up, waiting for a time in the future to deal with? What do you need to help you to deal with it now? Is there anyone in particular you need to speak with?

I find that if I go through several days in a row feeling increasingly discouraged and despondent, then I'm not taking enough time to pray or to reach out and ask for help. It's amazing how transforming a few words of encouragement and insight can be from another member of the body of Christ!

---

*Dear Lord, forgive us when we get so caught up in our own lives that we forget we are part of your body, and that you are able to refresh and restore us. Help us to remember that we are not on our own. Amen*

**CR**

# Falling out

*The disagreement became so sharp that they parted company;*
*Barnabas took Mark with him and sailed away to Cyprus.*

Paul and Barnabas had done an amazing work, sailing around Asia Minor preaching the gospel of Christ. Now Paul wanted to revisit the places where they had stayed, to see how the infant Christian communities were getting along. Barnabas suggested taking Mark, but Paul rejected the idea because Mark had abandoned them on an earlier voyage. They argued so fiercely that they fell out. Barnabas went one way with Mark, and Paul went another with Silas. The two men who had been so close through a host of adventures allowed a disagreement to break their partnership.

Inevitably, there will occasionally be differences of opinion and strong feelings between Christians, but the challenge is to model ourselves on the example of Christ, who commanded honesty, self-knowledge and radical obedience to himself. Am I sticking faithfully to a matter of principle, or am I being pigheaded? Is my aim to serve the body, or am I seeking something for myself?

We do not hear much more about Barnabas, and it seems that Luke, the writer of Acts, travelled on with Paul. Who was right? Under the circumstances, was their parting of the ways the best way forward? We don't know the answers to these questions, but we know that both men carried on serving God.

---

*Dear Lord, forgive us when we argue, and help us to find a way forward that brings honour to you. Help us to forgive one another and ourselves. Amen.*

*Read Matthew 7.*

                                          **CR**

# Adapting our behaviour

*Paul wanted Timothy to accompany him; and he took him and had him circumcised because of the Jews who were in those places, for they all knew that his father was a Greek.*

What a price Timothy had to pay for being considered acceptable to the Jews he and Paul were trying to reach! This is typical of Paul; he didn't let *anything* stand in the way of reaching people with the message of the gospel of Christ.

I often reflect upon what it is about my lifestyle that might put off those to whom I am trying to minister. If I am meeting with people from the media, is my style likely to increase or decrease my credibility in their eyes? If I am talking with my neighbours, do I understand and empathize with the local issues?

Paul is famous for saying 'I have become all things to all people, so that I might by any means save some' (1 Corinthians 9:22). He was prepared to do anything, as long as it wasn't a sin, in order to catch people's attention for the sake of Christ. He went out of his way to relate to those he met and inspire them to trust him.

Our constant aim should be to emphasize what we have in common with others, and not draw attention to what separates us. Strong personal preferences and cherished traditions should not become stumbling blocks between us and other people. Instead, we should go out of our way to minimize the differences and maximize the reality of what Jesus Christ can do in all our lives.

---

*Lord, forgive me when I care more about my own style and way of living than in bringing your transforming life to those I meet. Help me to see others with your eyes of compassion and love. Amen.*

*Read 1 Corinthians 8 and 9, or Romans 14.*

**CR**

# Being obedient to the vision

*During the night Paul had a vision: there stood a man of Macedonia pleading with him and saying, 'Come over to Macedonia and help us.'*

When I was in my early twenties I had a vision about living and working with women in Europe, with a sense that I would be used to influence their lives and faith in God. At the time, I was still living in America, and I had not yet met my future husband, Chris, so I had no idea I would soon be moving to England.

A few years later, with two young children, I became caught up in the day-to-day existence of running a home and being a full-time mother. It was only after my daughters started school that I was reminded of the vision. At last, it began to make sense, and I was ready to follow where the Lord was leading me. I became involved with groups that ministered to women across the country, and I was increasingly asked to write and speak at various events. The vision I had had years before began to unfold, and it continues to unfold even now.

Not everyone has a strong sense of what it is they're meant to do for God, but they know the peace of God as they put one foot in front of the other and walk in faith. Others may have a clear and burning sense of what they have been called to do. One thing is certain, whether the way ahead is clear or clouded, all disciples of Christ are asked to stay close to the One in whom there is all life and strength for the way ahead.

---

*Dear Lord, you have called us to be your own beloved children. Please help us to live our lives drawing ever closer to you. Amen.*

*Read John 15:5–17.*

CR

# Seizing the opportunity

*On the sabbath day we went outside the gate by the river, where we supposed there was a place of prayer; and we sat down and spoke to the women who had gathered there.*

Paul had an open mind when it came to winning people for Christ! He could have set his cap at influencing only the high and mighty, or just targeting the religious establishment, but he responded to the Spirit freely as he travelled and met people.

One of the people who heard what he was saying about Jesus was Lydia, a wealthy business-woman who sold a sought-after purple dye. She already had some sort of faith in God, and when she listened to Paul, the Lord 'opened her heart' and she was baptized, along with the rest of her household. She was so eager and hungry to learn more that she persuaded Paul and his friends to come and stay at her house.

A small congregation started meeting at her house, and it was to this group that Paul later wrote his letter to the church at Philippi. The 'chance' en-counter between Paul and Lydia went on to bear much fruit, and resulted in a new Christian community being founded.

Only God can see clearly the hungry hearts and open minds of the people we meet. It is up to us to reach out to others in love, and ask the Holy Spirit to guide us to those who will be receptive to the message of Christ. We can't imagine what has been happening in the lives of those we meet, but we can be confident that the Lord will show us how to bring God's love and promise of new life to the people we encounter.

---

*Dear Lord, help us to know when we are to speak of you, and give us the courage and wisdom to do so with grace. Amen.*

**CR**

# High adventure with the Holy Spirit!

*But when her owners saw that their hope of making money was gone, they seized Paul and Silas and dragged them into the marketplace before the authorities.*

Paul sure had a knack of getting into hot water! This time he made himself deeply unpopular with the owners of a slave girl who could tell fortunes. The spirit that was in the slave girl kept on calling out that Paul and his friends were servants of the Most High. Paul became annoyed, and cast the spirit out of the girl in the name of Jesus Christ.

The owners were furious and dragged Paul and Silas before the magistrates, who had them stripped, beaten and thrown into prison. In the night an earthquake shook the prison, and the chains that had been tied around the prisoners became undone and all the prison doors opened. The jailer was so frightened of what would happen to him that he took out his sword to kill himself. Instead of letting the jailer commit suicide, Paul stopped him and explained that they had not escaped. The jailer clearly sensed a greater power at work, because he immediately asked how he could be saved. He then took Paul and

Silas and treated their wounds and had Paul baptize him and his entire household.

What an extraordinary incident! Once again, Paul does not react the way most people in his situation would. Instead of running for his life in the confusion of the earthquake, Paul stayed to reassure the man responsible for keeping him in prison.

Paul's reaction was that of a person transformed by the Holy Spirit. How could I transform some of the hopeless-seeming situations in my life if I really believed that the Holy Spirit was up to the task?

---

*Dear Lord, please help me never to limit your power in my life. Amen.*

**CR**

# Not colluding with wrong

*But Paul replied, 'They have beaten us in public, uncondemned men who are Roman citizens, and have thrown us into prison; and now are they going to discharge us in secret? Certainly not! Let them come and take us out themselves.'*

The morning after the night of the earthquake, the magistrates sent word to have Paul and Silas released. But Paul was having none of it! He reasoned that if they, as Roman citizens, had been thrown into prison unlawfully, then they were not about to slink out as if they were real criminals.

Paul refused to collude with the magistrates' mismanagement of the situation, and insisted that if he and Silas were free to go, then the magistrates would have to come and convey that message themselves. So the magistrates came to Paul and Silas and apologized for how they had been treated, and politely asked them to leave.

Only someone who is certain they are in the right can afford to behave like that! I have been aware at times of colluding with other people's mistakes and shortcomings, and allowing embarrassing details to be swept under the carpet. Sometimes I wonder if I am too quick to smooth over problems that really should be faced and dealt with.

It is one thing to ease someone's unintended mishaps, but quite another to collude with deliberate bad practice. Each of us needs the wisdom and intuition of the Holy Spirit to know how to respond when we have the choice to collude or call to account.

---

*Dear Lord, help us to know when to stand up for what is right, and when to forgive and forget. Amen.*

*Read Matthew 10:16–20.*

**CR**

# Battling jealousy

*Some of them were persuaded and joined Paul and Silas, as did a great many of the devout Greeks and not a few of the leading women. But the Jews became jealous, and with the help of some ruffians in the marketplaces they formed a mob and set the city in an uproar.*

How many of us can lay our hands on our hearts and swear that we have never acted out of jealousy? Whether it was a barbed comment, a significant silence or a full-blown smear campaign, have we been entirely free from succumbing to the green-eyed monster?

Jealousy is a hateful emotion which can twist our hearts as well as our minds. Even when we don't *do* anything, feeling jealous can distort our perceptions and rob us of our peace.

The times when I have been jealous of someone else, I have no idea if my jealousy ever affected them, but I know for certain how it hurt me. It made me feel small and shrivelled and impotent, as if I had lost all my own good attributes. I think my jealousy was part of being frightened: frightened of losing someone, frightened of not measuring up, frightened of being frozen out. There have also been times when I have been the object of other people's jealousy, and their actions have made my life miserable.

The reality is that jealousy is part of the sin from which we have been delivered in Christ. We need to stand against jealous feelings, confess them if we harbour them, and ask God to forgive those who are jealous of us. Unlike Paul, we may never have to fight for our lives, but we may have to fight to restore a damaged reputation or relationship.

---

*Dear Lord, in your mercy deliver us from jealousy. Amen.*

*Read 2 Timothy 1:7.*

**CR**

# What do I know about my faith?

*While Paul was waiting for them in Athens, he was deeply distressed to see that the city was full of idols. So he argued in the synagogue with the Jews and the devout persons, and also in the marketplace every day with those who happened to be there.*

Paul was able to join any group of people and give well-argued reasons for his views and beliefs.

One of the paradoxes of the Christian faith is that its central message of God's love and our salvation through Jesus Christ is so clear and resonates so profoundly with the human experience that everyone who hears it ought to be able to respond in some way. However, delving deep into the 'why' and 'how' of the Christian faith is a theological voyage that could take a lifetime! Theologians may have carefully thought-through explanations for everything to do with the Christian faith, but that still doesn't mean that they've been able completely to dissect or analyse God!

At the heart of our faith remains a mystery, the mystery of who and why God is the way God is, and no amount of study can dispel that mystery. Ultimately, God can only be understood through a relationship of love. At some point, we have to put down our books and reach out to God as a person who will always be in some way beyond our precise understanding. But as in any relationship of love, the more one loves, and allows oneself to be loved, the closer one becomes to the other.

We should all have the confidence to ask questions about our faith so that we, in turn, can answer questions about our faith, but we must do so realizing that the surest way to draw close to God is to open ourselves to his overwhelming and never-ending love for us.

---

*Dear Lord, help us to love you with our heads as well as our hearts, and show us the truth about you through the Holy Spirit. Thank you. Amen.*

*Read 1 Corinthians 13.*

CR

# Old truths, new insights

*Now all the Athenians and the foreigners living there would spend their time in nothing but telling or hearing something new.*

I love reading through the Sunday papers, glancing at the fashions and other photographs and picking out a story or bit of news that interests me. One colour supplement has a 'diet of the week' column, and it never ceases to amaze me how many new ways there are to lose weight and stay fit. However, most of the diets seem to revolve around a few basic principles, to which the latest scientific discovery, or passing fad, is added.

The description of the Athenians as people always itching to hear something new reminds me of the diet of the week: what they heard last week is old hat, and only the latest craze will do. The problem with continually changing a set of beliefs (or a diet!) is that there is no chance for follow through, for really putting the thing to the test.

While it must always be possible to gain new insights and learn new ways of thinking about our faith, the core of what we believe does not change. Our understanding may grow and deepen, and over a lifetime may alter significantly, but that is not because God changes—it's because we change!

Our challenge is to remain open to God, to the teaching and insight of the Holy Spirit, while holding fast to the core teaching of our faith. This is, of course, where Christians differ and disagree, sometimes violently. This is why we need our theologians, our prophets, our teachers and women and men of prayer, and each of us needs to pray continually that we will walk in the way of God's eternal truth.

---

*Dear Lord, help us to know what to believe about you and about life, and in your mercy keep us growing ever closer to you. Amen.*

*Read 2 Corinthians 5:16–21 and Hebrews 13:8.*

**CR**

# A common starting point

*Then Paul stood in front of the Areopagus and said, 'Athenians,
I see how extremely religious you are in every way. For as I went
through the city and looked carefully at the objects of your
worship, I found among them an altar with the inscription,
"To an unknown god." What therefore you worship as unknown,
this I proclaim to you.'*

How far do you think Paul would have got with the Athenians if he had begun by criticizing their religious expression? They would have switched off completely, and written him off as a pompous windbag. But Paul was clever. He could see that they were fascinated by religious issues and he started by complimenting them on their interest. He then proceeded to expound upon the nature of the God they had declared 'unknown', building up to a teaching about Jesus Christ.

This is such a good example for us today. How many times have you found yourself in a conversation where the subject turns either to horoscopes, faith healing or other areas dealing with spirituality? Did you commend your friends for their interest in non-materialistic things, and gently build towards speaking from the Christian perspective, or did you tell them they'd got it all wrong?

It isn't always easy to make our voices heard in this relativistic and pluralistic age, but it is possible. After all, if we have a well-thought out and compelling perspective on life, others will be intrigued by our opinions. What will probably speak louder than anything is our attitude and our confidence in our own faith. What is more, people can sense the Holy Spirit, even if they don't know who they are sensing! If I speak about what I believe to be true, then God can speak to people's hearts and draw them into his truth.

---

*Dear Lord, I feel helpless a lot of the time in the face of so many other points of view. Please help me to stay close to you so that when I do speak about you others will sense that I am speaking about someone who is real. Amen.*

*Read Ephesians 3:14–21.*

**CR**

# Dionysius and Damaris

*But some of them joined him and became believers, including Dionysius the Areopagite and a woman named Damaris, and others with them.*

At the very end of Acts, chapter 17, Luke records the names of two individuals who became Christians—Dionysius and Damaris. We know that Dionysius was a member of an ancient and prestigious court in Athens, and one early source states that he later became bishop of Athens and went on to be martyred. There is, as far as I can tell, no further mention of Damaris. Why she was singled out for mention is lost to the obscuring mists of history.

Whoever she was, it is obvious she made an impression on Luke, and no doubt on Paul as well. Was she, like Lydia, particularly wealthy and generous? Was she highly intelligent or well connected? Whoever she was and whatever she did, it was sufficient to gain her inclusion in Luke's history alongside another person who became an outstanding Christian.

You and I may never become even footnotes in history, but we can be confident that our lives count. They count because we are beloved of God, and we live and move in his strength and power. It may not feel like that to us most of the time, but that is our reality. Each of us has what it takes to make a difference in the lives of people around us, although we may never know what effect we have had on anyone!

This is why I think we should take more risks with God's love. Who can you contact today with a message of support and encouragement? Who needs to see you and have you put your arms around them? What action do you believe you must do for the sake of the kingdom—today? What are you doing in response to God's love for you? How can you express the joy of being a citizen of heaven?

---

*Dear Lord, thank you for creating me and showing me your love and mercy. Inspire me to pass them on to others. Amen.*

*Read Romans 7:6 and Romans 8:11.*

**CR**

# Give thanks

*O give thanks to the Lord, for he is good; for his steadfast love endures for ever.*

When things are going well, we often hear people say, 'God is good'. But when things are not going quite so well? Is God still good? Our perception of things is partial and dim. God sees the whole picture. Sometimes he may permit difficulties and trials to bring us to repentance or to strengthen our faith. We may not perceive this to be 'goodness' at the time, but God is looking ahead to the finished product. He is looking to our highest, ultimate good, rather than our passing pleasure. His goodness is not dependent on our subjective appraisal of it. Goodness is part of his character. Recently a friend of mine, who has known much suffering and bereavement, wrote to inform me of the death of her 'beloved friend'. In her grief, she concluded her message with these words: 'God is good. This is still my testimony.'

God's goodness is expressed through deeds—*good deeds*—or actions. And this psalm brings to our notice some of these expressions of God's goodness. It is addressed first and foremost to God's people, Israel. Written in the context of Israel's history, it refers primarily to Israel's deliverance from exile. God has 'redeemed' his people (v. 2)— bought them back from the enemy—and gathered them to himself (v. 3). And that really is something to give thanks for! The apostle Peter tells us that we too have been redeemed— bought back—'but with the precious blood of Christ'.

The first verse of Psalm 107 also mentions God's 'steadfast love'. Love too must be demonstrated. And what is the highest, fullest expression of God's love to us? The apostle Paul wrote to the Christians in Rome: 'God demonstrates his own love for us in this: while we were still sinners, Christ died for us' (Romans 5:8, NIV).

---

*While we were still sinners— totally undeserving of his love— Christ died for us. What a cause for thanksgiving!*

**BA**

# Desert wastes

*He satisfies the thirsty, and the hungry he fills with good things.*

Following the three verses of introduction, which we looked at yesterday, Psalm 107 gives us four illustrations of ways in which God has redeemed his people. The first one, in verses 4–9, is of those who are lost, homeless. They 'wandered in desert wastes'. What a horrible picture of nothingness, and lostness. The 'inhabited town' (v. 4) would be a place of refuge, where they could settle and put down roots. But, in contrast, they wander. They have no roots, no security, no place to call their own. They are dying of hunger and thirst and distress. What a scene of hopelessness and death.

But in their despair they know where to turn. We read in verse 6: 'Then they cried to the Lord in their trouble, and he delivered them from their distress.' Maybe somebody reading these notes is 'wandering in desert wastes', figuratively speaking. Why not cry out to God for deliverance?

How did God deliver these lost, homeless wanderers? 'He led them by a straight way' (v. 7) in contrast to all their aimless meanderings. God gave direction to their lives. 'He led them by a straight way until they reached an inhabited town'— that place of security and refuge, where they could put down roots and belong. They are encouraged to 'thank the Lord for his steadfast love, for his wonderful works to humankind. For he satisfies the thirsty, and the hungry he fills with good things' (vv. 8–9). They find well-being and fulfilment in the Lord, in whom all needs are met.

---

*To those wandering in desert wastes, who have lost their way, Jesus says, 'I am the way.' To those who are hungry, Jesus says, 'I am the bread of life.' And to the thirsty and tired, he is the living water and the giver of rest. 'Come to me,' he says, 'all you that are weary and are carrying heavy burdens, and I will give you rest' (Matthew 11:28).*

**BA**

# Prisoners

*He shatters the doors of bronze, and cuts in two the bars of iron.*

We come to the second illustration of those who were far from God—'prisoners in misery and in irons'. Again a terrible picture of the suffering of those who are shackled 'in darkness and in gloom' and whose 'hearts were bowed down with hard labour' (vv. 11–12). Verse 11 tells us they were in this state because 'they had rebelled against the words of God, and spurned the counsel of the Most High'. Their condition was aggravated by the fact that 'there was no one to help' (v. 12). Utter solitude, loneliness, helplessness. No one to reach out to them in their need. They can only stumble in the darkness, trapped in the gloom of their condition.

They took the only way out. 'They cried to the Lord in their trouble, and he saved them from their distress' (v. 13). God hears the cry of despair. He sets the prisoner free. 'He brought them out of darkness and gloom, and broke their bonds asunder' (v. 14). Prison gates and bars are nothing to God.

These words are reminiscent of the prophecy recorded in Isaiah 9. The previous chapter concludes on a sombre note of 'distress and darkness, the gloom of anguish' (Isaiah 8:22). Then chapter 9 begins with a tremendous contrast: 'But there will be no more gloom for those who were in anguish... The people who walked in darkness have seen a great light...' and goes on to prophesy the birth of Jesus, who came into this world to dispel the darkness and set the prisoners free.

I recently read about a young Englishman, who came to know the Lord while in prison in Sri Lanka. Although he died in chains in 1999, he had found true freedom in Christ, for Jesus says, 'If the Son makes you free, you will be free indeed' (John 8:36).

---

*Are you imprisoned—by sin, addiction, a dependency problem, a relationship problem...? Turn to God. He can break your chains and set you free.*

**BA**

# Affliction and healing

*Some were sick… he sent out his word and healed them.*

In verses 17–22 we have a different picture of rebellion, resulting this time in sickness. Notice again that those who were afflicted brought their troubles upon themselves. It was 'through their sinful ways' (v. 17) that they were sick. Sin has its consequences, one of them being that 'they loathed any kind of food' (v. 18). They were ill and unable to eat, their lives had become so disordered.

It is so sad that people seem determined to get hurt—to hurt themselves—through turning their backs on God. Here they are 'near to the gates of death' because of their rebellion. But they too know where to turn. We read: 'They cried to the Lord in their trouble' (v. 19). They needed healing and God 'sent out his word and healed them' (v. 20).

In the New Testament we see Jesus, the Word made flesh, going about healing people. In the case of the centurion's servant (Matthew 8:5–13), the centurion says to Jesus, 'Only speak the word, and my servant will be healed.' And 'Jesus said, "Go; let it be done for you

according to your faith." And the servant was healed in that hour.' That's the healing power of God's word. We know from the epistle to the Hebrews that 'the word of God is living and active, sharper than any two-edged sword, piercing until it divides soul from spirit, joints from marrow; it is able to judge the thoughts and intentions of the heart' (Hebrews 4:12).

If only those who rebel against God, bearing the terrible consequences of their sin, would cry out to him in their distress, he would rescue them and bring healing, as he does in this psalm. 'He delivered them from destruction' (v. 20). Another wonderful picture of redemption!

---

*'Let them thank the Lord for his steadfast love, for his wonderful works to humankind. And let them offer thanks, giving sacrifices, and tell of his deeds with songs of joy' (vv. 21–22).*

**BA**

# Calamity

*He made the storm be still... and he brought them to
their desired haven.*

Here we come to our fourth picture, a terrifying one of those caught in a raging storm at sea. In December 1999, France was devastated by storms, the like of which had never been seen before. People were killed. Whole forests were flattened by gale force winds: three hundred million trees were damaged. Hundreds of thousands of homes were without telephones and three million homes were without electricity. Off the coast of Brittany an oil tanker split in two, causing an ecological disaster. The TV news showed the unleashed fury of the waves as they battered that boat. We saw then in reality, what is depicted in this psalm: the littleness and weakness of man against the mighty, destructive forces of nature.

In our psalm the tempest is the work of God: 'He commanded and raised the stormy wind, which lifted up the waves of the sea' (v. 25). Then we have a glimpse of man's stark fear in the face of this particular danger: 'Their courage melted away in their calamity; they reeled and staggered like drunkards, and were at their wits' end' (vv. 26–27). And what do they do? By now we can anticipate this refrain: 'They cried to the Lord in their trouble' (v. 28). And once again he acts: 'He made the storm be still, and the waves of the sea were hushed... He brought them to their desired haven' (vv. 29–30)—a place of security, calm, peace, shelter, refuge, protection, safety.

---

*This reminds us of another storm—on Lake Galilee—when a similar thing happened. It was evening and Jesus and his disciples were crossing the lake in a boat. The wind rose to gale force and soon the waves were swamping the boat. Terrified, the disciples woke Jesus who was asleep in the back of the boat. He rebuked the wind and told the sea to be still. The wind dropped, and 'there was a great calm' (Mark 4:35–39).*

**BA**

# True riches

*He turns a desert into pools of water, a parched land into springs of water. And there he lets the hungry live, and they establish a town to live in; they sow fields, and plant vineyards, and get a fruitful yield. By his blessing they multiply greatly.*

The four pictures we have looked at this week, illustrate the places from where the redeemed have been gathered (vv. 2–3). All these people, who were far from God, he delivered—from danger, from bondage, from death and destruction—and gathered them in to be his people. 'Once you were not a people, but now you are God's people' (1 Peter 2:10).

All of us can find ourselves somewhere in these pictures, because all of us were separated from God through rebellion, through sin. And God responded to our cry and 'made him who had no sin to be sin for us' (2 Corinthians 5:21, NIV). Jesus paid the price of our rebellion; he bought us back, redeemed us with his own precious blood. 'For it is not God's will that any should perish', the Apostle Peter tells us, 'but that everyone should come to repentance.'

This redeeming God transforms situations. He is sovereign. He is judge—the *righteous*

judge. In verse 34 we read that it was 'because of the wickedness of its inhabitants' that God 'turns rivers into a desert, springs of water into thirsty ground, a fruitful land into a salty waste'. But in the verses that follow, God turns poor resources into fertility.

Surely this should be a warning to us not to put our trust in material wealth, which can so easily give a false sense of security. 'For you say, "I am rich. I have prospered, and I need nothing,"' we read of the church in Laodicea. 'You do not realize that you are wretched, pitiable, poor, blind and naked' (Revelation 3:17).

*True riches are found only in Jesus. 'You know the generous act of our Lord Jesus Christ, that though he was rich, yet for your sakes he became poor, so that by his poverty you might become rich' (2 Corinthians 8:9).*

**BA**

# Gladness

*Let those who are wise give heed to these things, and consider the steadfast love of the Lord.*

This final verse of our psalm encourages us—if we are wise! —to see ourselves in the four previously-examined pictures, to realize our own need and count on the steadfast love of God. It makes the whole psalm intensely personal and practical. It is not only the story of a long-ago, far-off people, it is also up-to-date and relevant for us today. It is not just superb poetry; it also reflects our own experience. We should be open to the lessons the psalm teaches. We are to apply them and benefit from them.

Perhaps there is also a warning implicit in these concluding verses. It is so easy for us, once things are going well, to forget all about God. It seems as if that may have happened here for we see from verses 39 and 40 that after tremendous blessings and fulfilment, fortunes are reversed. We need constantly and consciously to depend on God. Verse 41, however, begins with that word, which is so little but so important, the word 'but', signifying a radical change: '*But* he raises up the needy out of distress.'

In the four illustrations which form the body of this psalm, it is only as the different groups of people recognize their need that they are able to turn to God and cry to him in their trouble. In each case, 'he saved them from their distress'. This is still true for us today. If we in our lostness, darkness, sickness and sinfulness turn to God and cry out to him, he will immediately reach out to us and save us. For did not God come into the world in the person of Jesus Christ for that very reason? In Matthew's Gospel, we read that Mary would bear a son, and that he would be called Jesus, 'for he will save his people from their sins' (Matthew 1:21).

---

*'The Son of Man came to seek out and to save the lost' (Luke 19:10).*

**BA**

# Creative hands

*Come, let us sing for joy to the Lord… In his hand are the depths of the earth, and the mountain peaks belong to him. The sea is his, for he made it and his hands formed the dry ground. (Psalm 95:5)*

*In his hand is the life of every creature and the breath of all mankind. (Job 12:10)*

*Your hands shaped me and made me… Remember that you moulded me like clay. (Job 10:8–9)*

I am writing this on a secluded beach in Devon. Getting here involves a long hike and a risky climb down the cliffs, so there are no ice-cream kiosks, deck chairs or beach huts; absolutely everything I can see was made by God himself. I could probably count a million of them if I had powerful binoculars and a microscope. Gulls soar over the towering cliffs behind me, gigantic cumulous clouds drift overhead and the sea sucks gently round the rocks. I've spent the afternoon enjoying the rock pools, fascinated by all the different colours of the seaweed, anemones and the tiny darting fish. Even the little stones between my toes all have their individual shapes.

So few ever come here that all this staggering beauty exists almost exclusively for God's pleasure. Why not, his hands made it—but does the Almighty have hands? Did he roll the earth into a ball in his palms and fling it into orbit? Well the Bible tells us he not only has palms but our names are tattooed on them (Isaiah 49:16). David, the shepherd, tells us it was God's fingers that made the moon and the stars (Psalm 8:3). And God himself says, 'My own hands stretched out the heavens' (Isaiah 45:12). God is so powerful that he can create anything merely by a word of command, but perhaps he uses the word hands because he longs to make it easier for us to identify with him.

---

*Thank you, Father, that you have the whole world in your hand.*

*'Father, into your hands I commit my spirit' (Luke 23:46).*

JRL

44

# Loving hands

*It was not by their sword that they won the land, nor did their arm bring them victory; it was your right hand, your arm, and the light of your face, for you loved them.*

Recently I sat holding my mother-in-law's hand as she peacefully slept her way into heaven. As I thought about those hands, now so still but in the past so constantly active, I wondered how many acts of love they had performed during their 86 years: caring for her disabled mother, feeding, washing and changing her three babies—and my six! All those birthday cakes they had decorated; delicious puddings that ruined all my diets; mountains of ironing and washing-up they had worked through and the many grazed knees and elbows they had tended. She was always shy about expressing her love in words, but her hands said it all!

Hands are so expressive that it is not surprising people in Old Testament days often linked God's hands with his love and care. Ezra the priest did it often when he wrote his astonishing account of how he led thousands of Jewish captives back to their homeland over a bandit-infested desert.

'The king had granted him everything he asked, for the hand of the Lord his God was on him' (Ezra 7:6). 'I was ashamed to ask the king for soldiers and horsemen to protect us from enemies on the road, because we had told the king, "The gracious hand of our God is on everyone who looks to him…" So we fasted and petitioned our God about this, and he answered our prayer' (Ezra 8:22–24). 'Because the hand of the Lord my God was on me, I took courage' (Ezra 7:28). 'On the twelfth day of the first month we set out… to go to Jerusalem. The hand of our God was on us, and he protected us from enemies and bandits along the way' (Ezra 8:31).

---

*Lord, thank you that you promise to cover me, today, with the shadow of your hand (Isaiah 51:16).*

**JRL**

# Overshadowing hand

*The Holy Spirit will come upon you, and the power of the Most High will overshadow you.*

Perhaps the phrase 'the hand of the Lord' means something different to each of us. Certainly this was so for two Bible contributors who both used the term often. For Ezra, having God's hand with him meant guidance and protection, but for Ezekiel, it meant something totally different. He lived in Babylon, where he and his fellow Jews had been dragged as captives after their nation's defeat. They were living in isolated ghettos all over the vast empire. Ezekiel was an itinerant prophet, travelling constantly between the groups, teaching and encouraging. As he wrote his book, he looked back over many years of ministry, but certain moments stood out vividly. They were times when he felt God's presence so strongly that he often fell to the ground. They were so important to him that he recorded the date and described exactly where he was (by the Kebar River, in the village of Tel Abib, or in his own home).

Obviously Ezekiel felt that the Holy Spirit was overshadowing him like a giant hand as he heard God speak and was shown prophetic pictures. Modern psychologists would describe this as an altered state of consciousness and theologians might say he was 'slain in the Spirit'! But for Ezekiel they were the vital milestones in his life.

Can you remember times when you felt God came very close to you?

We do not know how it felt for Mary, when the 'the power of the Most High overshadowed her', but something supernatural happened, for God himself began to grow inside her. Something is planted in us, too, when God comes to us in those private and special moments, whether we fall to the ground dramatically, like Ezekiel, or simply feel a supernatural calm in the middle of one of life's storms.

---

*Could you make a list of your own 'God encounters'? Note where they happened, what you felt like, who else was involved and how they changed you.*

**JRL**

# Holding hands

*For I am the Lord, your God, who takes hold of your right hand
and says to you, 'Do not fear; I will help you.'*

We shake hands to express friendship, to 'make up', or to cement a business deal—and what about the thrill of holding hands with someone you love? Obviously hands are a very important part of relationships.

Some of the children I used to foster had been so badly treated that they found it very hard to trust adults. One small boy had been regularly tied into his bed for 16 hours at a stretch. His body was covered with bruises and festering sores and the way he cowered away, when I tried to touch him, was heartbreaking. I don't think he had ever seen the sea, so when we took all the children for a day on the beach he became rigid with terror at the sight of the waves rolling towards him. Suddenly a cold, clammy hand was thrust into mine. All day he clutched my hand tenaciously, refusing to let it go even if that meant eating his precious packet of crisps with his left hand!

By the afternoon, his confidence had grown enough to allow him to run with me through the sandy puddles left by the retreating tide. His little legs had never been given the chance to run and jump before, so he often stumbled. 'You won't let me fall, will you?' he would say anxiously. 'Keep hold of my hand—promise?'

That day changed him. Gradually he became a normal, happy child, but it was the action of grabbing my hand that began our relationship. God's top priority with us is our relationship with him. He longs for us to grab his hand like that, whenever we feel afraid, lonely or confused.

---

*'My soul clings to you; your right hand upholds me'* (Psalm 63:8).

*'If the Lord delights in a man's way, he makes his steps firm; though he stumble, he will not fall, for the Lord upholds him with his hand'* (Psalm 37:23).

**JRL**

# Warning hands

### *The Lord's hand has gone out against me!*

Suddenly, round the corner, a policeman appeared holding up his hand. As I jammed on my brakes, he shouted, 'There's been an accident, you'll have to go back.'

While we all enjoy the comforting verses about God's hands protecting and guiding us, there are also many that describe his 'hand against' individuals or nations. Sometimes God says, 'If you don't get out of this relationship... stop this habit... this activity... you'll be in danger of losing your integrity... your spiritual health... people you love.' We can then choose to stop, or go on regardless of the consequences. There are also several references to God's hand being heavy, rather as a father's hand might feel heavy to his disobedient offspring!

When we ignore God's hand of warning, and allow some temptation to become a way of life, his punishment does not always fall in this life. God's grace is so enormous that he gives us time for repentance, but these days we are dangerously inclined to think that God is *all* love and *only* love. He *is* love, of course, but he is also righteousness. He cannot overlook sin, because it hurts innocent people: justice has to be done, so every sin we ever commit has to be punished, ultimately. When we repent, Jesus himself takes that punishment for us, but there are Christians who find a particular sin so attractive that they prefer to continue in it, rather than repent and change. The sin robs them of God's favour and blessing that they once enjoyed, but they refuse to recognize consequences such as guilt and loss of peace as 'God's heavy hand' on them. The book of Hebrews says some very serious things about Christians like this.

---

*'If we deliberately keep on sinning after we have received the knowledge of the truth, no sacrifice for sins is left... The Lord will judge his people. It is a dreadful thing to fall into the hands of the living God'* (Hebrews 10:26, 30–31).

*Is there a 'danger area' in your life?*

                              **JRL**

# Appreciative hands

*You will be a crown of splendour in the Lord's hand, a royal diadem in the hand of your God.*

Crowns are usually associated with heads rather than hands! But as I turned this verse over in my mind, I realized that you can't see a crown if you are wearing it. You have to hold it in your hands to enjoy it to the full. You need to feel the smoothness of the gold, and turn the jewels in the light to see them sparkle. Most of us have such horribly low self-esteem that the idea of God gaining pleasure from looking at us feels bizarre! We often develop a low opinion of ourselves in childhood. Adults called us stupid, clumsy, bad or difficult, and we grew up labelled by these invisible names. In Isaiah 62:2, God promises to change our name (that is, our identity). He is in the business of changing people, and goes on to say in verse 4, 'No longer will they call you Deserted, or… Desolate. But you will be called Hephzibah (The Lord is delighted with you).'

We *can* think differently about ourselves when we see how *God* thinks about us!

So what great things do we have to achieve in order to become this treasure that the Lord holds so proudly? It is not a question of what we do but how we react to what others do. Pearls are formed when a grain of sand gets into the oyster's shell, irritating its soft body until it wraps the sand round with the protective layers which, later, form a valuable jewel. Diamonds are created only after years of pressure. Gold has to be exposed to intense heat so that all the impurities surface and can be skimmed off (see Job 23:10). Accepting, without bitterness, the heat of life's traumas, grinding pressures or endless small irritations is what forms, what God calls our 'treasures of darkness' (Isaiah 45:3).

---

*Lord, help me to realize that all these problems that weigh me down can be transformed by you into something beautiful which will one day give you great delight.*

**JRL**

# Guiding hands

*If I make my bed in the depths, you are there… if I settle on*
*the far side of the sea, even there your hand will guide me, your*
*right hand will hold me fast. If I say, 'Surely the darkness will*
*hide me and the light become night around me', even the darkness*
*will not be dark to you; the night will shine like the day,*
*for darkness is as light to you.*

Life can sometimes feel frighteningly dark, can't it? We feel lost and not sure which way to turn. David, who wrote this psalm, felt like this often, but he assures us that God's hand was always there to guide him through frightening or confusing situations. Our foster daughter, Jane, was seven when she came to us. Her father had died suddenly that day; she had lost her mother through cancer a couple of years previously.

At first she settled quite well, but then the panic attacks began. The first one literally paralysed her with fright during a school firework party, but soon they happened anywhere.

One day I took her shopping. She was chattering happily as we walked along the crowded pavement together, when a car backfired behind her and triggered an attack. This time she was not rooted to the spot: she ran wildly, heading straight for the busy road, blinded by terror.

Diving after her, I caught her— just in time. She did not respond to my comforting words: I had to take her somewhere safe, but she was too big to carry. So, holding her unwilling hand very tightly, I guided her rapidly between the crowds of shoppers in the direction of the park. There, on a bench, I rocked her in my arms until she was peaceful again.

I know, now, how horrible panic attacks feel, when life suddenly loses all its landmarks, familiar structures and special people, leaving you feeling lost and confused. But God's guiding hand is there, and he won't let us take a wrong turn.

---

*Please hold my hand today, Lord.*
**JRL**

# Rejected hands

*All day long I have held out my hands to an obstinate people,*
*who walk in ways not good, pursuing their own imaginations—*
*a people who continually provoke me to my very face.*

Our friendly church was being changed into a battleground by a violent disagreement. Friends were transformed into enemies overnight and the pain we were inflicting on each other was staggering. Matters were coming to a messy head in the church meeting. I sat in tears as I looked round the room, loving people on both sides. Suddenly, I lost my cool and, standing up, I told them all to stop behaving like spoilt children and breaking our Father's heart!

The following Sunday I was on 'welcome duty' at the church door, which meant shaking hands with everyone. I stood there with my welcoming smile and my hand held out, but, one by one, people from both sides walked past me, ignoring my hand. I had probably asked for it by being tactless, but these were old friends, some of whom I'd led to the Lord, and others were members of my own house-group. It all blew over in a few weeks, but every time I read the verse at the top of this page, I remember the agony I felt that morning.

The more we love someone, the greater is their capacity to hurt us by their rejection, so God must feel infinitely worse than I can imagine when so many of the people for whom he died ignore him completely.

---

*Lord I know you hold your hands out to me, too, all day long. I almost hear you say, 'Come and sit with me a while,' but I switch on TV. 'Tell me how you're feeling, share this worry with me,' but I ring a friend. 'Why don't you ask for my help?' But I stress myself out, trying to solve the problem myself. 'Come and let me hold you,' but I open a packet of biscuits for comfort. Please forgive me for ignoring your outstretched hands so often.*

**JRL**

# Jesus' hands

*As the eyes of slaves look to the hand of their master...*
*so our eyes look to the Lord our God.*

During the last few days we've been looking at some of the references to God's hands in the Old Testament. Perhaps they have seemed rather abstract, but we can all identify with the hands of Jesus and it is by watching them that we learn most about the character of God.

We only have our imaginations to go on for his first thirty years, and many delightful but fictitious stories are told about the way his childish hands mended birds' wings or broken toys. However, we are given a generous list of things his hands actually did during his last three years. Not only did he lay them on the sick but he wrote in the dust, washed feet, served meals and even cooked a beach barbeque.

His hands must have been strong, skilful, suntanned and roughened by years of manual work. They were also incredibly gentle and tender. Mark remembers how Jesus used a child as an illustration for his quarrelling disciples. He didn't just point him out to them from a safe, adult distance: 'He took a little child (by the hand) and had him stand among them. Taking him in his arms, he said to them, "Whoever welcomes one of these little children in my name welcomes me"' (Mark 9:36).

Mark also tells us how Jesus bent down and lifted a child to his feet after an epileptic fit. The child's father was there so Jesus could easily have left him to care for his son, who had been writhing on the filthy ground in his own dribble, urine and, possibly, vomit. Instead, Jesus himself reached down to restore his dignity, perhaps wiped the little boy's mouth and smoothed the sweaty hair from his bewildered eyes, before taking his hand and lifting him up.

---

*Thank you that you don't expect me to clean myself up when I've been on the ground. Your hands reach down to me in the mess where I am.*

JRL

# Dirty hands

*Filled with compassion, Jesus reached out his hand and touched the man. 'I am willing,' he said. 'Be clean!'*

It amazes me to realize how willing Jesus was to get his hands dirty. This is particularly remarkable in days when people who were considered holy washed their hands repeatedly throughout the day (Mark 7:1–6) and wouldn't even permit the shadow of a prostitute to fall on their path. They held their cloaks tightly when they walked through a crowd in case they brushed someone who was 'unclean'—the disabled; those with skin diseases or discharges; lepers and menstruating women. Yet Jesus, who had the power to heal by 'remote control', often touched people like that.

He was nearing a village one day when he met a funeral procession. In the middle of the crowd of wailing women, one face looked so agonized that 'his heart went out to her' (Luke 7:13). She was the mother of the young man who had just died, and he was all she had left in the world.

'Don't cry,' said Jesus softly. He could have raised the corpse with a word, like he did for Lazarus; instead he put his hand on the coffin and the bearers stopped amazed, because touching a corpse also made you unclean.

Jesus is not high above the ugliness of grief; he's right there in the centre of it.

Another time his path was blocked by the grotesque figure of a kneeling leper. The disease causes the flesh of its victims to be eaten away, leaving them covered with infectious and disfiguring sores. 'You could help me, if you wanted to,' the man said. Because lepers were outcasts, considered lowest of the low without status or rights, maybe he didn't feel the kind of person Jesus would bother to help. The hand of Jesus was the first that had touched him in years! (Luke 5:12–13).

---

*Lord, sometimes I, also, feel I'm not 'quite the right sort of person' for you to want to help. When I think like that, help me to remember how you touched that leper.*

**JRL**

53

# Generous hands

*You open your hand and satisfy the desires of every living thing.*

Jesus often used his hands to give. The one who had voluntarily given up ownership of the entire universe had no money or possessions to share, but when a small boy gave him his picnic lunch Jesus immediately gave it away to the hungry people surrounding him (John 6:9–13). His hands multiplied his own personal supply of food like that on a number of occasions.

The only other thing Jesus could give was his blessing. When mothers eagerly approached him, longing for him to pray for their children, the disciples rudely shooed them away. Mark tells us, 'Jesus was indignant, 'And he took the children in his arms, put his hands on them and blessed them' (Mark 10:16). Don't we all long to see his hands touching our own children like that!

On the first Easter Sunday evening, a couple asked him to supper. Because they were traumatized by the crucifixion, they did not recognize him until he stretched out his hand to give them a piece of bread during the simple meal. The nails had left that hand so horribly bruised and distorted that they recognized him instantly (Luke 24:30–31). That story always moves me to tears, and so does this one: the host at a Jewish festival meal used to dip a piece of bread in the sauce and hand it to the guest he honoured most highly. Just minutes after Jesus had used his hands to wash the feet of Judas Iscariot, he also handed him this special 'sop'. He already knew what Judas planned to do that night, so was he offering him one last chance to save himself from being labelled as the worst traitor in history? (John 13:18–30).

---

*Could you stop for a moment and picture those wounded hands reaching out to you? Ask him what they are offering you: a chance to change; the opportunity to know him better; blessings for your family; some new spiritual gift or anointing for service; the daily bread—ordinary necessities—that you need today?*

**JRL**

# Restoring hands

*So he went to her, took her hand and helped her up. The fever left her and she began to wait on them.*

I can remember lying in bed fuming during my eight years of illness, when I often had to listen helplessly to my husband and children creating chaos in the kitchen below. Illness, disability, loss and old age rapidly sap our confidence, making us feel marginalized. Was this how Peter's mum-in-law felt, the day a very special visitor came for a meal? One touch of his hand and she was up, dressed and busy in the kitchen! Jesus does not always restore health, youth or mobility but his touch always restores hope and gives us a reason for living. His servants are never on 'the sick list' and never retired. Serving him may not mean doing the active, practical jobs, but the words 'worship' and 'serve' are the same in Hebrew. Do you need his hand to restore your ability to enjoy his company and intercede for others?

Who else but Peter would have jumped out of a boat on a stormy night, walked a few steps on the water, and then panicked! Matthew says he yelled, 'Lord, save me!' Immediately Jesus reached out his hand and caught him (Matthew 14:30–31). Have you ever felt you were drowning in problems, worries and confusion? Peter was never safer than at the moment when he felt most afraid, because it was then that Jesus reached out to hold him. It was merely Peter's faith that needed restoring.

The hand of Jesus can also restore life. When an agitated father hurried Jesus through the crowds to his daughter, who had just died, Jesus took her hand, and she lived! (Mark 5:41).

---

*Is there an area of your life that has died—your faith, hope or creativity; the love or respect you once had for a husband, parent or child? Has your joy died, killed by despair? Has your peace been strangled by worry? Could Jesus be holding out his hand to you, longing to restore life to that dead place?*

**JRL**

# Healing hands

*People brought to him a man who was deaf and could hardly talk, and they begged him to place his hand on the man. After he took him aside, away from the crowd, Jesus put his fingers into the man's ears. Then he spat and touched the man's tongue. He looked up to heaven and with a deep sigh said to him, 'Ephphatha!' (which means, 'Be opened!').*

During eight years of illness, I read all the Christian books on healing, desperately trying to discover the secret formula that would make me well. Some 'experts' claimed that healing comes through the laying on of hands, while others insisted it's all down to deliverance, lengthy prayer counselling, or being 'slain in the Spirit'. Finally I concluded that there isn't a formula: Jesus worked differently with each individual.

Tracy finds crowds very confusing because of her deafness; often she can't understand what is happening. I wonder if that is how the man in today's story felt when the crowd dragged him to Jesus. They wanted to see a miracle: how cross they must have been when Jesus took him by the hand and walked off with him!

Jesus knew it would terrify the man if he suddenly heard the noise of an excited crowd after hearing nothing all his life.

Rather than startle him, Jesus used his hands to communicate what he was doing by sign language. He put his fingers in the man's ears, touched his tongue, looked up to indicate he was praying and then spoke a single word which would have been easy to lip-read.

I wonder what people at a healing service would think if, instead of administering the 'laying on of hands' at the communion rail, the vicar started spitting in their eyes and mouths!

---

*Thank you, Lord, that you treat us all as individuals. May I never try to put you in a box, tied up neatly with academic ribbons and theological bows. I don't understand why you heal some and not others, but I know you do not require me to understand you, only to trust you.*

**JRL**

# Helpless hands

*When they came to the place called the Skull, there they crucified him… Jesus said, 'Father, forgive them, for they do not know what they are doing.'*

We have been looking at some of the things which the Bible tells us were done by the 'hands that flung stars into space' (Graham Kendrick). Surely the most incredible of them all was their apparent helplessness when thugs nailed iron stakes right through them. How did Jesus feel as those cruel, mocking faces hovered over him and the hammer blows began? He was no longer considering escape; he had already battled out that issue in Gethsemane (Luke 22:42). Rage or fear could be expected at a time like that, but it was love that he felt, love for the men who were torturing him and love for you and me, as he allowed himself to take the punishment which should have been ours.

Was there was something that hurt even more than those hammer-blows? The helplessness he felt during the hours that followed must have been terrible. When those active, generous hands were pinned to the cross, apparently useless, he must have longed to wipe the tears from his mother's face and reach out to comfort his friend John. I guess we can all identify with that sense of helplessness as we watch our child plunging headlong into a destructive relationship or course of action—when he or she is too old to be grabbed and pulled back to safety; or the helplessness we feel as we watch the person we love dying in pain or when someone else is destroying our marriage. It is always a comfort to know that Jesus understands how we feel, but in actual fact he was *not* helpless. He *could* have stepped down from that cross, but he chose not to. We are not helpless either. Praying, which can seem so inactive, may actually be the very best way to help other people.

---

*Lord, I refuse this suffocating sense of helplessness as I watch these people I love. I choose, instead, to fight for them by prayer.*

**JRL**

57

# An exciting start

*As soon as Jesus saw them, he called them; they left their father Zebedee in the boat with the hired men and went with Jesus.*

Recently I went to a lovely wedding, where the beautiful English bride was marrying a charming Dutchman. We all glowed in their reflected happiness, and wished them well, especially since the new wife would have to get used to living in another country, and learning a new language. This didn't appear to bother her though—she would follow her new husband because she loved him, and deal with any difficulties using the strength that love gave her.

James and John must have felt something rather similar. To be prepared to leave their families, their jobs, their security, and follow Jesus into the unknown must have demanded much more than just curiosity or a thirst for adventure. They were the next generation of the family business, and their father was going to miss them. But for something as special as this it was worth it.

I wonder if our relationship with Jesus is still like that of the young bride or the new disciples, fresh and exciting, with every day bringing thrilling discoveries? Or has it settled down into boredom and duty, with a feeling that something important is missing? If that's the case, then to do nothing is to allow something glorious to fade away. After all, Jesus didn't say 'Follow me, and I will fill your life with interminable meetings' or 'Follow me and I will teach you how to sleep through the sermon'!

If we keep close to Jesus though, we will feel the same sense of excited anticipation that the disciples knew. They walked with Jesus every day, they discussed, prayed, argued, suffered, laughed and failed in his presence, and marvelled at the things they saw him do. Perhaps today, we could talk the day through with him, as events unfold, and look at his world with a sense of wonder at what he shows us.

---

*Help us to be eager to follow.*
**WP**

# Take a risk

*And Jesus said to them, 'Follow me and I will make you become fishers of men.'*

I doubt if Simon Peter and his brother Andrew had any idea what Jesus meant by this, or how he was about to turn their lives upside down. They knew, though, that to refuse his invitation would be the biggest mistake they could make. So they accepted the challenge, and began to let him transform them from unremarkable fishermen into his confident and capable agents.

Today's reading was the text for the sermon at my confirmation service, when I was made a full member of the church. I was thirteen, and my most vivid memory of the service was that I was wearing what I regarded as an unflattering dress, and looking particularly dumpy. My faith didn't really ignite until my last week at school, when I was challenged by a group of friends. If I really believed that Jesus was raised from the dead, and was therefore alive now, what difference did it make to me? I struggled with this all night, because I was convinced that if I let God have some control in my life, he'd send me as a missionary to South Africa, and I didn't feel up to that!

But I finally had to take the risk, just as the disciples did. As it turned out, I think God knew that I wasn't missionary material! He's had some challenging things in store for me, but all in some way 'good'. There are times when we say a resounding 'No' to God, for fear of him leading us into the unknown, lacking confidence in ourselves and in God. But God knew what the disciples were capable of, and he knows what we can become too. He can see the gold buried deep within us, even if we can't, and he would love us to trust him enough to let him guide us into our future.

---

*Is there something that God is wanting to lead you into?*

**WP**

# Unconditionally loved

*Jesus left that place, and as he walked along, he saw a tax collector, named Matthew, sitting in his office. He said to him 'Follow me.' Matthew got up and followed him.*

Matthew was not used to good people actually talking to him. He'd got used to being ignored, avoided, pointed out to the children as an example of someone gone bad. He worked as a customs official, something no Jew who wanted to obey all the rules about purity could do, so he was despised as unpatriotic. But then, he wasn't poor as so many others were—he'd made his choice, and he could live with it most days, as long as he didn't think about it that much.

He'd heard of Jesus, of course, and he'd even dreamed of lurking anonymously at the edge of the crowd to listen. Then Jesus turned his world inside out: 'Matthew, follow me.' What on earth was going on?

Jesus didn't say, 'Matthew, if you make a stupendous effort to reform, prove that you're a new man, then I'll let you sneak in at the back.' Matthew was in his office—he was still doing his job, an unreformed character— when Jesus called him. He was called first, and reformed later.

We often get this the wrong way round in our lives. A lovely lady once told me that she prayed a lot for other people, but wouldn't ask for anything for herself, as that would be presumptuous as she wasn't a good enough person. We need to learn that God sees not just what we are, but what we can become, and that it's he who changes us, and not us by our own efforts. Whatever we are at the moment, we are good enough for God. So if you are disappointed in yourself, if you feel you are always getting it wrong, remember that Jesus put no preconditions on his call to Matthew—and Matthew got up and followed him.

*Thank God that he loves us as we are.*

**WP**

*Luke 9:1–2 (NRSV)*

# Relying on God

*Then Jesus called the twelve together and gave them power and authority over all demons and to cure diseases, and he sent them out to proclaim the kingdom of God and to heal.*

When I was a student, I was talked into going on a mission in Hull. The churches there had been working towards this for a long time, planning and praying, as had the students. We eventually descended on this unsuspecting town, filled with a mixture of enthusiasm and terror, but determined to do our bit for God, and leave no soul untouched. I marvel now at the patience and generosity shown to us by the mature and forgiving Christians of Hull, as we babes in the faith either blasted our way through all doubt, or shrunk away in a corner trying not to be noticed! We learned a vast amount about ourselves, and the need to rely totally on God.

Jesus knew what was good for people, which is why he sent the disciples out before they probably thought they were up to it. I can hear them asking for more time to study, or pleading that they were too inexperienced for anyone to take them seriously. But we learn from our mistakes, and the best way to get closer to God is to rely on him for help. We are much more comfortable doing things we know we can do, trusting only in our own ability, and leaving God out of it. We need to tackle the difficult stuff, for which he alone can give us strength. Or if we are stuck with doing something we've done lots of times before, then we need to make a special effort to hand it over to God, to let him make it seem new. If we pray for a new challenge, we need to be aware that God answers prayer!

---

*Pray for God's strength for someone (maybe yourself) facing a difficult challenge.*

**WP**

*Mark 6:30–31 (NRSV)*

# Take a break—if you can!

*The apostles gathered around Jesus, and told him all they had done and taught. He said to them, 'Come away to a deserted place all by yourselves and rest a while.' For many were coming and going, and they had no leisure even to eat.*

Do you recognize this scenario? The disciples had been sent out by Jesus, all had gone amazingly well, and now they were so busy they could hardly think. Success breeds success—you only have to give one good talk and the phone never stops ringing with requests for more! You only have to be a good listener to one needy soul, and somehow the whole world thinks you have the time and ability to listen to them! The phone always rings at meal times, because that's the only time you're in, and all of a sudden you're resenting all these demands on you and wishing you'd never got involved in the first place.

Jesus knew the value of a time apart, and he taught the disciples to at least try to build some space into their lives. He was good at finding the quiet place to be alone. But if you read on a little, these verses are the lead-in to the feeding of the five thousand. The crowd wasn't going to leave these wonderful people alone that easily, and they rushed on foot round the lake to reach the other shore before Jesus and the disciples got there. Instead of complaining about them, Jesus taught them, and fed them. There is a difficult balance to be maintained here, and we need to be flexible. Jesus and the disciples did manage at other times to have time alone, to rest and to relax. But when faced with people in need, Jesus showed by example what to do. Our task is to try to get the balance right, and to enjoy the busyness of life as well as the stillness.

---

*Lord, teach me to enjoy what life brings, and to keep my life in balance.*

**WP**

# The cost of discipleship

*Then he said to them all, 'If any want to become my followers, let them deny themselves and take up their cross daily and follow me. For those who want to save their life will lose it, and those who lose their life for my sake will save it.'*

No one could accuse Jesus of not giving it to them straight. Not a great way of enticing people to be disciples, we may think—no promises of good health, happy family life, promotion at work, or plenty of money. But the disciples were all prepared to try it, and go down the road of possible suffering, self-denial and surrender to God. At the end of Peter's life, tradition has it that he asked to be crucified upside down, because he was not worthy to meet the same death as his Lord. Had it all been worth it for the disciples? We need only to open the Bible on any page of Acts to find that it was!

But how seriously should we take Jesus' words today? We may not be asked to face persecution, but self-denial isn't too nice either! As I write this, my husband is climbing the highest mountains in England, Scotland and Wales, in 48 hours, with an intrepid group of (younger and fitter) volunteers, to raise money for youth work. This has involved fitness training—going up and down our three flights of stairs fifteen times a night—and now climbing in the cloud and rain. I'd hate it! But they wouldn't be able to do this without the training, and that's what we must do as disciples. Every little act of saying 'no' to our desire to put ourselves first, 'no' to our resentment of others, 'no' to our fear of commitment, is an act of training towards the goal of finding our truly glorious life in God.

*Lord, help me to see if there is something I should be working on in my training.*

**WP**

# Putting your foot in it

*Peter spoke up and said to Jesus, 'Teacher, how good it is that we are here! We will make three tents, one for you, one for Moses, and one for Elijah.' He and the others were so frightened that he did not know what to say.*

Peter brings hope to those of us who writhe in embarrassment at some of the stupid things we've managed to say. Here was a completely mind-blowing incident, where Jesus' clothes had become dazzling white, and he appeared to be talking to the long-dead Moses and Elijah, representing the law and the prophets—a great visual confirmation of who Jesus was. In this situation, most people would keep their mouths firmly shut! But not Peter. If there was an awkward silence, Peter was just the man to fill it. He made the totally inappropriate offer to build three tents for Jesus, Moses and Elijah. Maybe Peter was trying to make permanent a vision that could be only temporary, or maybe he was once more speaking first and thinking second!

Have you had similar times when what you've just said has made you feel stupid? For those of us who have problems remembering people's names and faces, there's the classic, 'Could you just remind me of your name, your face looks so familiar?' 'Certainly, it's Jenny—you had dinner with me last month.'

Then there's the old favourite, 'It's lovely to see new people in church.' 'Actually I'm not new, I've been coming for twenty years.' Do you wonder how God could possibly have patience with someone who can get it so wrong? Then remember that Jesus built his church on Peter.

Perhaps you have been on the receiving end of some well-meaning but unintentionally hurtful comment? We are sensitive beings and easily hurt. Remember that despite Peter's ability to put his foot in it, Jesus still loved him, and saw the good inside.

---

*Help me to forgive myself when I say stupid things, and to have patience with others.*

**WP**

# Back to reality

*A man in the crowd answered, 'Teacher, I brought my son to you because he has an evil spirit... I asked your disciples to drive the spirit out, but they could not.'*

Jesus, Peter, James and John had just come back from the 'mountain top' experience of the transfiguration, and immediately found argument and failure. The disciples left behind had been attempting to heal an epileptic boy, and were making a mess of it. Back to reality with a dull thump! Have you noticed how often this happens? You've just been to a really inspiring talk, and come home ready to set the world alight, only to find that the cat's been sick, or the oven hasn't turned itself on, or your daughter thinks she's failed her exams. It's easy to leave the world behind when we're singing uplifting hymns, but reality is waiting to engulf us as soon as it can!

The disciples had to face this too. Living every day with Jesus, they still couldn't escape real life, and now their failure to heal the epileptic boy was giving the scribes ample opportunity to belittle them, and cast doubt on Jesus' choice of them.

So what's the answer when the world swamps us with its ordinariness? How do we cope when we're interrupted every few minutes, and all the good things we planned to do that day just fail to happen? How do we recapture our closeness to God when the dinner is burning and the phone is ringing? The mountain-top moments may not happen often, but recalling them when life gets tough can help to refresh us and give us confidence. We just have to get on with life, remembering that Jesus and the disciples knew all about tough living—God is as close to us in everyday life as he is on the mountain-top.

---

*Try to remember the times when you felt that God was especially close.*

**WP**

# What gives us status?

*Then James and John, the sons of Zebedee, came to Jesus.*
*'Teacher,' they said, 'there is something we want you to do for us.'*
*'What is it?' Jesus asked them. They answered, 'When you sit on*
*your throne in your glorious Kingdom, we want you to let us sit*
*with you, one at your right and one at your left.'*

James and John, together with Peter, formed the inner circle of Jesus' disciples. They were always there at important moments, and maybe thought of themselves as being rather special. They'd given up a lot for Jesus, and done their very best to do what he wanted. So surely, when all worked out well in the end, some reward was in order? This was not some unrealistic pious group of devout characters, but a group of ordinary people just like us, with natural ambitions. They believed in Jesus' greatness with all their might, and they wanted some recognition for their devotion.

James and John received the gentle reply that only God could sort out the end times, and that in the meantime, the ones who were the greatest were the servants of others. Wow! That turns the world's values upside down, doesn't it? Our marks of status, like our shiny new car, our good job, our smart clothes, our responsibili-ties in church, our being popular, might give us confidence but are not what makes us great in God's eyes. It's what's inside —our attitudes towards others, our desire for their good, our willingness to put other people first. On that basis, however successful we may seem, we have a lot further to go. Even James and John, who listened to Jesus daily, hadn't got it right.

Then what about ambition? God has given us abilities in order to use them, and as long as we know where our true status lies, then we're free to show the world that Christians are good at things too!

---

*Help me, Lord, to remember where true greatness lies.*

**WP**

# Peter's denial

*Peter answered, 'I will never leave you, even though all the rest do!' Jesus said to Peter, 'I tell you that before the cock crows twice tonight, you will say three times that you do not know me.'*

Peter the enthusiast, the impetuous, the man of action, the leader, was about to meet his biggest test. Over-confident perhaps, and certainly unprepared for the terrible fear and danger he was about to encounter, but totally devoted to his Lord, and in theory anyway, prepared to risk everything for him. Peter was one of the two who followed Jesus, who tried to stay close despite the risks, whilst the other disciples faded into the night. So Peter started off well.

Do you remember the disgrace of the cricket captain last year who had to admit that despite being a much respected and admired Christian, he had been involved in taking bribes to fix matches? We hear of cases where the church treasurer has been less than honest with the finances or where the organist has run off with the vicar's wife. And it's not just something that happens to other people. We all have the possibility of over-confidence, of taking the easier way out of trouble, of manipulating the truth a bit if it makes life easier, of lashing out without thinking, of ignoring our principles.

And what makes it worse is that Peter had been warned, so he should have been on his guard. Sometimes we are so caught up in the present, that we find it hard to stop and look objectively at what we are doing. But take heart. Jesus did still found his church on this glorious failure of a man, and sometimes through failure we start to see ourselves with more realism and humility. Then Jesus can get to work on the real person, and not an imaginary superhero we could never really be.

---

*Lord, help me not to be crippled by my failures, but to know they give you a way of re-making me.*
**WP**

# Peter's second chance

*When they had finished breakfast, Jesus said to Simon Peter, 'Simon, son of John, do you love me more than these?' He said to him, 'Yes, Lord; you know that I love you.' Jesus said to him, 'Feed my lambs.'*

I know of an upright, gracious man whose daughter got involved with drugs, and was arrested in a remote country on suspicion of drug dealing. He braved the hazardous journey out to visit her, stood by her, and welcomed her back into the family home when the charges were eventually dropped. He glows with joy and pride when he talks about her, how she's trying to start afresh, and how wonderful it is to be re-making their relationship. That's how God is with us.

Peter had probably tried to put his denial of Jesus to the back of his mind, pretending to himself that it didn't matter that much. But Jesus knew that Peter needed to face his failings and really experience forgiveness, right in the core of his being. So when the right time came, Peter was given his chance. Peter had to look into the eyes of Jesus, and say boldly that he loved him, three times over to mirror the three denials, three times over so that the experience became real and not just in his head. We can believe theoretically that we're forgiven, but we need really to experience this, like the daughter did when her father arrived at her cell, or like Peter when he looked straight into Jesus' eyes.

Forgiveness has consequences though. Peter was to 'feed my lambs'—to look after those who would be caught up into this life-changing movement, to tell them what had happened to him, to assure them that God's love was for them too, and that it was never too late to start again.

---

*In a time of quiet, try to look into the eyes of Jesus. Know that he sees you as you really are, let him forgive you, and give you a fresh start.*

**WP**

# Thomas the outsider

*So the other disciples told him, 'We have seen the Lord.' But he said to them, 'Unless I see the mark of the nails in his hands, and put my finger in the mark of the nails and my hand in his side, I will not believe.'*

Thomas was not with the others when Jesus first appeared. Maybe he needed to have some space on his own to grieve for his Lord. Now he had a whole week of the other disciples talking non-stop about what the appearances of Jesus meant, whilst he felt out of it, isolated and confused.

It's easy to feel an outsider, and it hurts. I remember being driven home by the headmaster from school camp when I was ten because I'd caught mumps. The poor man had to put up with a weeping child for many hours. I was not particularly upset by the illness, but was mortified that I was missing out on what all the others would be doing. We can forget how difficult being an outsider is, and need to be reminded. Remember when you were a child in a new school, or an adult moving to a new area, or a newcomer in church?

We often label Thomas a 'doubter' as if doubt was something to be ashamed of. But Thomas was being honest: he knew that he couldn't feel convinced unless he'd had the same experience as the others. He didn't give up, opt out, shrink into himself or go back home! Thomas stayed where he felt most close to Jesus and talked to the others about what he was feeling. He didn't pretend to be all sorted out when he wasn't. He persevered and waited. And what a reward he got! Jesus knew what Thomas needed, and Thomas came through in the end with the greatest possible statement of faith—'My Lord and my God!'

---

*Look out for anyone who seems to be an outsider. Can you help them feel more at home?*

**WP**

# Transforming power

*God has raised this very Jesus from death, and we are all witnesses to this fact. He has been raised to the right-hand side of God, his Father, and has received from him the Holy Spirit, as he had promised. What you now see and hear is his gift that he has poured out on us.*

Here was Peter, who a few weeks before had been afraid to admit that he was a follower of Jesus, now giving the first Christian sermon to a crowd of over a thousand people. He was arguing persuasively and authoritatively, without any thought of his own safety, or of his lack of experience in public speaking. His message came straight from the heart, and his heart had just been set ablaze by the Holy Spirit. Now he knew the power of God within him and there was no stopping him!

It's very fitting that it was Peter who gave this sermon—the man who was never short of a word, a natural leader and spokesman. Yet Peter in his wildest dreams would never have imagined that he'd be up on his feet, exposed to public scrutiny.

The Spirit was a gift the disciples sorely needed. They'd seen their risen Lord, they'd got the head knowledge, but then what? They needed something to set them alight inside. Their questions must have been the same as ours today. How can we be different from our old selves, how can we have confidence, how can we live lives which show we know God in a special way?

We, like the disciples, have been given the gift of the Spirit, even if we've not experienced it in as dramatic a way as they did. We need to use this power, and not be afraid. It's when we risk using the gifts the Spirit gives, as Peter did, that we give him the chance to show us what he can do.

*Help me to let the power of the Spirit grow in me.*

**WP**

# Philip and the Ethiopian

*Now there was an Ethiopian eunuch, a court official... returning home; seated in his chariot, he was reading the prophet Isaiah... Philip asked, 'Do you understand what you are reading?'*

This is a great story, about Philip 'the evangelist', a later disciple. The official was a very important man, rich, influential and well educated. In modern terms he would be something like the Chancellor of the Exchequer in his Rolls Royce. He's waiting at the traffic lights, when a theology student, a bit untidy but full of enthusiasm, cycles up and asks if he understands the article he is reading. What presumption! Luckily there were no by-standers to die of embarrassment!

Instead of being put down, Philip found himself being lifted up, seated in the chariot, as man to man they had a deep theological discussion, just what the official had been longing for. Philip ended up baptizing this great man, who went on his way rejoicing.

I doubt if when Philip woke up that morning, he'd been expecting the day to turn out that way! But Philip was living each day open to God's guidance, and he'd been given the knowledge from God that this particular road carrying traffic to and from Africa was where he was supposed to be. He had no preconceived ideas of what he was to do—he just seized the opportunity that was presented to him. He asked a leading question, and left it to the official to respond. Philip didn't barge in where he wasn't wanted; he was invited in. I knew a young mum who, when her children were finally both at school, decided she had a little time on her hands. So for one week she resolved to pray that God would help her be open to any opportunities that came her way to do his work. She said she'd never had a busier week in all her life!

---

*Help me, Lord, to be on the look out for opportunities, and to respond to them sensitively.*

**WP**

# God's compassion and mercy

*He is merciful and tender toward those who don't deserve it;
he is slow to get angry and full of kindness and love. He never
bears a grudge, nor remains angry forever. He has not punished us
as we deserve for all our sins, for his mercy toward those
who fear and honour him is as great as the height of the
heavens above the earth.*

Compassion and mercy are not words we tend to think about much these days. We think more in terms of love, a word which has had its innate dynamic power replaced by sentimentality and inaction. Human compassion and mercy are active expressions of love for others that reflect the nature of God in whose image we are created. We often forget that God is merciful and compassionate; he can seem too big and far away to have characteristics like that!

Mercy actually means to have forbearance (patience) and a forgiving disposition towards one who is in one's power. Compassion means to have fellow feeling for the suffering and sorrow of others, to have pity on the unfortunate.

When we enter a living relationship with God the Father through Jesus Christ we get to know and understand that God is merciful towards us. God is not like man: he does not have to prove his power by being unyielding towards us. He has a forgiving disposition and is waiting patiently for us to help us in the difficult times we experience. He does not condemn us for our struggles, failure and difficulties; he feels for us in them… he is ultimately compassionate.

---

*Lord, we often forget you are merciful, that you deal with us patiently, and are always ready to forgive. Renew in us a fresh understanding of your nature so that we might not be hesitant about coming to you with our difficulties. Thank you that you feel for us in the sorrows we experience. Help us to acknowledge your presence with us today and every day.*

**AS**

# God's compassion and faithfulness

*Yet there is one ray of hope: his compassion never ends. It is only the Lord's mercies that have kept us from complete destruction. Great is his faithfulness; his lovingkindness begins afresh every day.*

The passage for today describes the feelings of someone who has had many years of suffering and has experienced grief that has brought them close to utter despair. However, the author is ready to acknowledge that the only ray of hope in their dire situation is the unending compassion of the Lord.

The Lord's compassion for us doesn't mean that he is always going to allow life to treat us kindly. We live in a world that brings sorrow and difficulty across our paths. We need to hold on to the knowledge that God is 'wonderfully good to those who wait for him' (v. 25). The Lord doesn't enjoy our affliction; he is compassionate and will show it (vv. 31–33). The things we suffer teach us much about ourselves and about the Lord. We need to make time to look back, listen and learn what it is he is trying to show us.

Verses 31–33 were recently on my desk calendar. Printed below them was the comment: 'The years teach us much that the days know little about.' When we are young in our faith, this can be hard to understand, because we haven't travelled very far in our walk with Jesus. As we continue to follow Jesus and the road stretches out behind us, we can see, that despite the difficult times, the Lord has been faithful, that the years we have followed him have taught us much that is invisible from day to day.

---

*A task: Take a piece of paper and divide it into eight sections. Ask the Lord to point out the milestones in your Christian life. Depict these in the first seven spaces, including relevant Bible verses. Leave the last space empty. Make time to ask the Lord to show you what he has planned next for your life. Fill in the space… and keep the paper where it can remind you of God's ongoing compassion towards you.*

**AS**

# The compassionate father

*So he returned home to his father. And while he was still a long distance away, his father saw him coming, and was filled with loving pity and ran and embraced him and kissed him… and said… 'We must celebrate with a feast, for this son of mine was dead and returned to life. He was lost and is found.'*

Our understanding of Jesus' and thus the Father's compassion for the lost is well illustrated in the parable of the prodigal son. The younger son has demanded his inheritance in advance, sold it and squandered the money far away from home, becoming destitute. Eventually things got so bad that the son decided that life at home as a slave would be better than what he had been reduced to. In a miraculous act of submission and humility he returns home.

The attitude of the father is the more amazing thing in this story. Most human fathers would have refused to give the son his inheritance in advance to start with. If a son sells his part of the family farm, it usually leads to anger and bitterness on the part of the rejected father. This son goes one step further and squanders the money rather than re-investing it. Everything is gone, never to be redeemed. Most human fathers would have disowned the negligent son by now, but not the father in this story.

This father has never given up having compassion for his son; his love is unconditional. The father is certainly hurt, rejected and disappointed, but never gives up hope that his son will come home again and is constantly watching out for him.

This is Jesus' picture of God the Father whom we have rejected and disappointed, whose compassion for his lost children is unending. He is constantly looking out for any sign that we may be heading back home into relationship with him.

*Think: nothing we do will make God the Father love us less. Nothing we do will make God the Father love us more.*

**AS**

# Jesus' humanity and compassion

*And it was necessary for Jesus to be like us, his brothers, so that he could be our merciful and faithful high priest before God... For since he himself has now been through suffering and temptation, he knows what it is like when we suffer and are tempted, and he is wonderfully able to help us.*

We have talked a little about the Lord's mercy and compassion towards us, but how can we be sure that he really knows what it is like to experience the things we do?

God the Father loves mankind with an unfathomable love, and to demonstrate that to us in a way that we could understand, he sent Jesus, his son, to earth to live among us and experience the daily trials and temptations that we face. That is how we can be sure that our situation is intimately made clear to God the Father in heaven, because Jesus, who mediates and pleads for us, has suffered in human flesh and had fellow-feeling for our situation.

Jesus knows what it is like to be homeless, an outcast, a refugee chased from his homeland to live in an alien culture, to go in fear of his life, to bear the stigma of illegitimacy, to lack possessions and be hungry, to be tempted, to lose a loved one. He experienced torture, misrepresentation, betrayal. He was falsely accused, branded a criminal and executed unjustly. The Bible tells us that he bore our sorrows and was acquainted with the bitterest grief (Isaiah 53). Nothing that any of us has experienced can be equated with that.

In addition, Jesus also took the burden of the sin of the world on his shoulders when he died on the cross and experienced being forsaken by God. He is therefore intimately acquainted with our human condition and wonderfully able to help us when we call upon him.

---

*Look up John 3:16 and learn this verse by heart.*

**AS**

*John 11:11–45 (LB)*

# Jesus sheds tears of compassion

*When Mary arrived where Jesus was, she fell down at his feet, saying, 'Sir, if you had been here, my brother would still be alive.' When Jesus saw her weeping and the Jewish leaders wailing with her, he was moved with indignation and deeply troubled. 'Where is he buried?' he asked them. They told him, 'Come and see.' Tears came to Jesus' eyes.*

When Jesus heard that his friend Lazarus had died, he travelled to the place he was buried and met Mary, Lazarus' sister. She was consumed with grief and probably indignation that Jesus had not arrived sooner. Jesus looked at the gathering; he saw Mary's grief and the professional wailing of the mourners and was moved with a compassion that welled up into indignation (v. 34) and anger (v. 38).

Jesus was not angry with himself for being late, nor with Mary for her emotions, nor the mourners for their lack of genuine compassion. He identified with Mary's grief, because he too had loved Lazarus, but he was indignant because he objected to the power that death had over people because sin had cut them off from the Father. Jesus' tears were as much for the plight of humankind as for his friend Lazarus.

We know that Jesus felt a very deep sense of compassion in this situation because the verb used when Jesus 'wept' is a different verb, with more intense feeling, that that used to describe Mary's grief or that of the other mourners. His compassion and indignation did not remain just an emotion; Jesus used this opportunity to raise Lazarus from the dead, demonstrating that he, Jesus, had power over death; because he would eventually show himself to be the Resurrection and the Life.

---

*Lord, thank you that your love for us is so strong that you feel anger at the power that sin and death has over mankind. Thank you, Lord, that your resurrection power is stronger than death. Give us the same indignation that you felt, so that by the power of your Holy Spirit we may constantly seek to bring people into your saving presence. Amen.*

AS

# Jesus shows compassion for the lost

*Wherever he (Jesus) went he healed people of every sort of illness.
And what pity he felt for the crowds that came, because their
problems were so great and they didn't know what to do or where
to go for help. They were like sheep without a shepherd.*

'Christ is the exact likeness of the unseen God' (Colossians 1:15). If we want to know what God is really like, we need to look at Jesus; his person, life and work. Jesus didn't just become man so that God could prove he understood our plight by going through the same problems as us, but so that we could see what God is really like... a compassionate and merciful Father.

In today's passage we see Jesus' reaction to the thronging crowds that flocked to see him and listen to him. He could see their innermost needs and their desperation and he felt compassion for them because they were lost, without anyone to guide and protect them. It would be easy to think that this was a 'pretty little feeling' that Jesus had, but the Greek word that is used here means 'it got him in the guts'. Jesus didn't think, 'Oh, the poor little lost souls!' but he was wracked to his inmost being over the plight of the people that God had created and who had fallen out of rela-

tionship with their Creator.

Jesus didn't only have a feeling; he did something. He told the disciples to pray for more workers to spread the Good News and then he chose twelve of them, filled them with the power of his Spirit and sent them out to preach and heal.

We learn from this passage the depth of God's compassion for us and that he is a God of action.

---

*Lord, give me a greater depth of understanding and compassion for the lost people in my family and community. Give me a burden to pray for them and a willingness to put into action what you lay on my heart. Amen.*

**AS**

# Jesus shows compassion for outcasts

*Once a leper came and knelt in front of him and begged to be healed. 'If you want to, you can make me well again,' he pled. And Jesus, moved with pity, touched him and said, 'I want to! Be healed!'*

Jesus also shows us by his example that God the Father is touched to the core by the outcasts of society. Here we see Jesus being moved with compassion for a leper. Leprosy is a terrible disease that eats away flesh. It is very contagious and those who developed leprosy were made to live outside society and were not welcome among the healthy and whole members of the community.

In our modern western society we don't meet lepers, but our culture has created the modern version of the leper, those we would rather not associate ourselves with. We could mention the mentally ill, the physically disabled, the homeless, and the emotionally needy. Some people would rather not be associated with anyone that didn't match up to their idea of 'the beautiful set' and so people are prejudiced against age, skin colour, size and religious belief.

The leper in the story was crying out, 'Lord, make me well... I want to be included in, I want to be loved and accepted! You can do it if you want to!' Jesus says, 'I want to! Be healed!' Apart from the challenge of believing that Jesus can still heal today, the challenge for us is… can we allow ourselves to be moved with the same compassion for today's social outcasts as Jesus was towards that leper? Are we willing to say to the Lord, 'I want to!' We needn't look much further than the next church pew or the corner of the coffee lounge for the outcast and the rejected.

---

*Lord, open our eyes to see the outcasts in our midst. Give us the courage to overcome our prejudices and show acts of mercy towards those who feel left out and rejected. Give us your love, wisdom and guidance in every situation. Amen.*

**AS**

# Jesus shows compassion for the sick

*Two blind men were sitting beside the road and when they heard that Jesus was coming that way, they began shouting, 'Sir, King David's Son, have mercy on us!' Jesus called, 'What do you want me to do for you?' 'Sir,' they said, 'we want to be able to see!' Jesus was moved with pity for them and touched their eyes. And instantly they could see, and followed him.*

In the Gospels we read about Jesus' compassion for the sick and how he healed people. What is interesting about this story is that the blind men shouted, 'Have mercy upon us!' They knew Jesus had power to heal them; they were at his mercy.

Jesus knew exactly what the blind men wanted him to do for them, but Jesus asked them, 'What do you want me to do for you?' Jesus wanted to hear with his own ears what they thought was in his power to grant them. 'We want to see!' they shouted. Jesus, moved with compassion, had mercy on them and touched their eyes. They were healed and followed him.

Recently a friend told me she felt the Lord was asking me, 'What do you want me to do for you?' At first I couldn't answer, I didn't think there was anything that I wanted God to do for me. Eventually I realized that I had lost sight of the fact that Jesus had the compassion and the mercy (power) to do even the most simple thing that, in my need, I asked for. We can all be like blind people sat at the edge of the road. When Jesus comes by, we are convinced that either our need or God's power is not great enough. We sit there, not daring to raise our voices.

Jesus has compassion on the physically, spiritually, emotionally and the mentally sick. We need to regain the realization that he has not only the compassion, but also the mercy and power to heal.

---

*Jesus says, 'What can I do for you? What can you do for others?'*

**AS**

# Jesus shows compassion for the needy

*One day about this time as another great crowd gathered, the people ran out of food again. Jesus called his disciples to discuss the situation. 'I pity these people,' he said, 'for they have been here three days, and have nothing left to eat. And if I send them home without feeding them, they will faint along the road! For some of them have come a long distance.'*

Jesus had already miraculously fed one large crowd (Mark 6:35–45) that had come out for the day without any food. Perhaps they had thought they wouldn't be there long and would be back in time for tea. However, the people had been so attentive to Jesus that before they knew it, they were hungry. Then Jesus multiplied the five loaves and two fish to feed 5000 men.

This time the crowds had come prepared. They had listened to Jesus for three days and now they had run out of food. Jesus felt compassion on them. He could see that they had been so keen to hear the truth of the kingdom that they had stayed longer than their food had lasted. Some of them had travelled a long way to listen to Jesus. He knew that without food they would faint along the road home.

Initially Jesus had been concerned because the crowd was spiritually lost. He now had compassion on them because in their desire to seek they had forgotten their practical needs. Jesus has compassion for both our spiritual and physical needs.

We must also learn to feel compassion for the needy and put it into action with acts of mercy. It is right to call 'helping the needy' an 'act of mercy', because in the affluent west we have the power to do something about the needs of the poor and the obligation to use that for others' benefit.

*Read Matthew 25:34–46. Think about practical acts of mercy you can do in your community and further afield.*

**AS**

# Jesus shows compassion for children

*Once when some mothers were bringing their children to Jesus to bless them, the disciples shooed them away, telling them not to bother him. But when Jesus saw what was happening he was very displeased with his disciples and said to them, 'Let the children come to me, for the Kingdom of God belongs to such as they. Don't send them away...' Then he took the children into his arms and placed his hands on their heads and he blessed them.*

Many of us have been brought up with the belief that 'children should be seen and not heard'. Many people feel it better if children are not seen at all! What the 'grown ups' are doing is too important to be interrupted by demanding children.

Women and children were among the least important in the Jewish society of the time. The disciples were sure that they shouldn't bother Jesus. But Jesus has a habit of up-ending all our social preconceptions and tells the disciples to let the children come to him.

Many times I have seen mothers with small children standing in the cold outside a church because there was nowhere else to go to escape the grimaces of the congregation. What must this say to these mothers, many who have come to church for the first time for a wedding or a christening?

Those of us whose small children are now older need to remind ourselves how it felt and be compassionate. It is too easy to think that our turn is over and we deserve some peace and quiet. But we are the ones who are in a position to help others in ways we would have liked. There are many acts of mercy that can be offered to allow small children and mothers to have a positive meeting with Jesus.

---

*Lord, give me compassion for small children and their mothers. Help me to remember that you welcomed and blessed children. Give me the grace to offer help to those who are struggling. Make us loving and welcoming. Amen.*
**AS**

*Luke 8:40–56 (LB)*

# Jesus shows compassion for the moment

*A messenger arrived from the Jairus' home with the news that the little girl was dead. 'She is gone... there's no use troubling the Teacher now.' Jesus said, 'Don't be afraid! Just trust me and she'll be all right.' ... Then he took her by the hand and called, 'Get up little girl!' At that moment her life returned and she jumped up! 'Give her something to eat!' he said. Her parents were overcome with happiness.*

I am one of those women who constantly struggle with balancing being a 'Mary' or a 'Martha', spending time with Jesus or doing what needs to be done. The 'Mary' attitude has been so exalted that we can get quite depressed if we feel our whole life is full of cleaning and cooking!

What I love about this passage is how Jesus juxtaposes the kingdom and the practical in almost one breath! First he raises Jairus' daughter from the dead and then tells the parents to feed her! We don't know how long the little girl had been ill, but she was probably very weak and dehydrated. Jesus knew that it was important the girl's physical need was met. It was not appropriate for her to sit prettily on her bed while he used the opportunity to teach the people!

It is good for us to learn that Jesus was not afraid to do what was appropriate for the particular moment, whether the act was of supreme spiritual significance or a small physical act of service in private. It can be as important to offer people a cup of tea as to offer them prayer. Preferably they should be offered both; in the order that fits the situation!

The compassionate and merciful heart listens to what God the Father is saying in each situation and acts accordingly. We have no need to constantly perform the spectacular to impress God or others... the Lord looks on the heart and our deeds are a reflection of its content.

---

*Lord, keep me from 'performance ministry'. Help me always to see with your eyes and act with your love. Amen.*

**AS**

# The business of compassion

*Then this message from the Lord came to Zechariah. 'Tell them to be honest and fair—and not to take bribes—and to be merciful and kind to everyone. Tell them to stop oppressing widows and orphans, foreigners and poor people, and to stop plotting evil against each other.'*

We have looked at the compassionate and merciful nature of God and how that is revealed through Jesus, giving us many examples that we can apply in our personal life and in how we relate to others. We have seen that compassion is not just a 'gooey' feeling that we get when we feel sort of sorry for someone, but a deep gut reaction, often born of our ability to identify with the sufferer through our own experience. We have seen that compassion is not just the ability to empathize, but to take action.

Like so many aspects of the Christian life, compassion is not an optional extra, it is an extension of the command to love our neighbour as ourselves. Obeying a command is a conscious decision of the will, it is not a matter of us waiting to be moved by emotion or the Holy Spirit, although he empowers us to carry the decision through.

Today's passage makes us look at taking compassion into the marketplace, the workplace and the corridors of power; cold calculating places. Those who move in such circles are often called upon to be tough… but the Lord calls us to be compassionate and merciful, and equates that with being honest and fair. It is very easy to take advantage of the powerless in society, but we have a God who commands that we see they get a fair deal.

---

*Lord, help me today in the difficult decisions I have to take, where showing your compassion may fly in the face of what is considered clever and to be expected in our secular society. Help me to be ready to give a good account as to what I have decided. Amen.*

**AS**

# Passing on help and comfort

*When others are troubled, needing our sympathy and encouragement, we can pass on to them this same help and comfort God has given us. You can be sure that the more we undergo sufferings for Christ, the more he will shower us with his comfort and encouragement.*

When my husband was training for the ministry, I belonged to a group of ordinands' wives who met for prayer, study and encouragement. I remember one meeting when everyone was very excited because one of the ladies was saying that the Lord had healed her of her post-natal depression. I remember thinking, 'Big deal, what's that anyway?' I was very young and had had no children myself, so I didn't understand why there was so much rejoicing. I had no understanding or compassion, no 'fellow-feeling' because the situation was beyond my experience.

Eight years later, I was that woman. I had had three babies in quick succession and a bad depression after the first two that was undiagnosed and thus untreated. Eventually I was confronted by my situation. The Lord opened 'a window of opportunity' and I opened myself to the possibility that he could change me; I wanted to be healed and whole. I was prayed for by a lovely lady and instantly healed. Although I still had much to learn, people could testify to the fact I was changed. As a result of this experience, I can now enter into the world of those who suffer in the same way. There is a frame of reference for 'fellow-feeling', compassion that wasn't there before. Such understanding and compassion leads us to be able to offer practical help also.

When we experience difficulties, we are better equipped to help others with the same problems and show them the compassion of Jesus by 'love in action'.

---

*What are the difficult things you have experienced? Ask the Lord to help you come to terms with these things enough to be able to show compassion and offer help to others in the same circumstances.*

AS

# Compassion, forgiveness and blessing

*And now this word to all of you: You should be like one big happy family, full of sympathy toward each other, loving one another with tender hearts and humble minds. Don't repay evil for evil. Don't snap back at those who say unkind things about you. Instead, pray for God's help for them, for we are to be kind to others and God will bless us for it.*

It is strange how people use the expression 'big, happy family'. Sometimes big families can be very unhappy because there is tension, no privacy, not enough individual attention when needed, restrictions, responsibility and resentment!

Domestic families and church families can experience this when individuals (grown ups and children!) allow themselves to become so self-orientated that the rest of the family begins to suffer. We occasionally have to 'read the riot act' to our family because sympathy, compassion, tenderness and humility have been chased out by unkind words, selfishness, retaliation and lack of consideration for others.

We need to ask ourselves why someone is behaving the way they are, and ask the Lord to give us the compassion we need to sympathize with that person, to forgive them and live patiently with them. More often than not, Jesus challenges us to be changed, so we can be a channel for growth. A more encouraging attitude in ourselves will gradually help the other person to change too. We mustn't wait for other people to make the first move... the Lord challenges us to be the compassionate peacemaker and as always with God, obedience brings a blessing all round.

---

*Lord Jesus, thank you for the challenge to be compassionate. Help us identify and root out the attitudes we have that are not compatible with living for you. Forgive us and help us to be forgiving that we might be a channel of blessing to others. Amen.*

**AS**

# Jonah, God's choice

*The word of the Lord came to Jonah son of Amittai: 'Go to the great city of Nineveh and preach against it, because its wickedness has come up before me.'*

Jonah came from a small Galilean village. Apart from this story, his one claim to fame is recorded in 2 Kings 14:25, when he prophesied that some land previously lost to Israel would be restored. 'Jonah' means 'dove', and if his nature matched his peaceable name, this man was a strange choice to send to the sophisticated and wicked Assyrian city of Nineveh—especially when the message was about the judgment soon to fall on them. But he was the person the Lord wanted and the book of Jonah teaches us about God's patience and mercy to him and to Nineveh, depite considerable human frailty and failure.

Time and again, the Bible tells how God called very ordinary people to tackle amazing tasks. He took shepherds like David, tax collectors like Matthew and young women like Esther, when all they had was their faith in his promises and the Holy Spirit in their lives. Often God's selections seem inappropriate—it appeared foolish to entrust the upbringing of the Son of God to an impoverished peasant girl—and didn't Jesus *realize* that Peter was decidedly rocky? Jonah was another curious choice, but God knew exactly what he was doing. 'The foolishness of God is wiser than man's wisdom, and the weakness of God is stronger than man's strength' (1 Corinthians 1:25).

God also has plans for you and me. We should always listen for his voice directing us to speak and act in his name. His ideas may not turn out as we envisaged and our 'word of the Lord' may be nearly as daunting as Jonah's. How will we respond?

---

*O Lord, I want to hear your word to me clearly. Help me be courageous in obedience, believing in faith and joyful in hope that you will use me to make a difference. Amen.*

**CB**

# Running away

*But Jonah ran away from the Lord... He found a ship...*
*After paying the fare, he went aboard and sailed for Tarshish*
*to flee from the Lord.*

Have you ever sensed God asking you to do something so difficult or embarrassing that your immediate instinct is to figure how to get out of it? For Jonah, being chosen to bring God's message of impending doom to Nineveh was his very worst nightmare. He probably felt socially inferior as a common Galilean before one of the most sophisticated and arrogant seats of power of that time. Besides, Israel considered heathen Assyria their enemy and Jonah would have had strong reservations about offering these pagans the chance of being saved.

Racism and prejudice are challenging issues today too. However much we try, our inbuilt fear, envy and lack of understanding of other ethnic, religious or social groups often makes it hard to accept everyone with the same openness and respect. Christians are not immune from this problem and sometimes we are guilty of judging individuals just because of their background. A neighbour of ours is a leading diplomat from a country where Christians are persecuted. I resented him living nearby, but one day we had a conversation. I learned about his wife and young children, how they found living in our street, and I warmed to this family who need to find Christ just like anyone else. We invited them to eat with us one day— perhaps the Lord will use this fragile relationship.

Jonah could not stomach God's instructions; preaching forgiveness and grace to undeserving, wicked people was not for him. He grabbed a bag and ran to the nearest seaport. 'No, Lord! I am *not* going to Nineveh. Here's my ticket—I'm out of here!'

---

*Do not let me judge by what I see; nor pass sentence according to what I hear; but to judge rightly between things that differ, and above all to search out and to do what pleases you, through Jesus Christ our Lord.*
THOMAS À KEMPIS

CB

# Sleeping through the storm

*Then the Lord sent a great wind on the sea, and such a violent storm arose that the ship threatened to break up… But Jonah had gone below deck, where he lay down and fell into a deep sleep.*

Teenageers, I'm sure you'll agree, are delightful to live with. But occasionally they have faults, like one we know, who is sometimes impossible to rouse. Tea, alarm clocks, loud music, threats, screams, cold water, all fail to bring him to an upright posture for long—he's soon snuggling back under the duvet.

Parents gain unique insights into how our heavenly Father deals with his children. Maybe Jonah was still a teenager himself—he exhibited all the signs. Just imagine the scene as the Lord sets about getting the attention of his comatose prophet. He could have given up and found someone else for the job (Jonah's sister? His mum?) but stayed relentlessly on his case, not in anger to show Jonah who was boss, but because he loved and longed to bless him. The storm God sent was capable of sinking the ship, striking fear into everyone. It came partly to shake Jonah out of his disobedience, to correct him. 'The Lord disciplines those he loves, and he punishes every-

one he accepts as a son' (Hebrews 12:6).

When God allows 'storms' into our lives, it is not necessarily because we need to be rebuked or humbled like Jonah. All Christians are called up to 'face trials of many kinds because you know the testing of your faith develops perseverance' (James 1:2–3). If you are in this place, ask God to reveal his love and give you the wisdom to face another day (v. 5). Perhaps others of us are asleep and need to wake up and listen to his word for our lives.

---

*Please speak to us, Lord— through the fire, the tempest or with that still small voice through it all. Awaken us to see your face and help us in our weakness.*

**CB**

# Jonah's confusion

*He answered, 'I am a Hebrew and I worship the Lord, the God of heaven, who made the sea and the land.' … (They knew he was running away from the Lord, because he had already told them so.)*

There is an old saying, 'He that would learn to pray, let him go to sea.' This storm certainly brought everyone to their knees, the crew and passengers crying out to all the gods they could think of. Jonah, conspicuous by his absence, was shaken awake by the captain, brought up on deck to join the prayer meeting, and soon had to explain himself.

I have a friend who won't display any Christian emblem in his car window in case his driving lets him down (I'm sure it never would!). Sometimes it seems easier not to mention our faith—maybe out of cowardice, or because we are exercising godly wisdom. Jonah, however, had already let the cat out of the bag: the sailors knew he was running away from God and he had certainly not spoken or acted in a way that brought honour to him.

We may wonder whether people notice or care that we are Christians, but I am sure they do, and watch like hawks when the pressure is on, to see whether our faith makes a difference. Jonah's confession, when it came, *was* honouring to the Lord, telling his hearers more about God than about himself—a mighty creator who held men to account but was merciful. The sailors took it in. Sometimes, like my motorist friend, we shrink from sharing about Jesus because we feel a poor advertisement for him. But God can reveal his true nature despite our shortcomings. Next time the opportunity arises, tell someone about the wonderful Saviour we worship.

---

*Do not fear what they fear; do not be frightened. But in your hearts set apart Christ as Lord. Always be prepared to give an answer to everyone who asks you the reason for the hope that you have.*

1 PETER 3:14–15

CB

# The sailors' salvation

*Then they took Jonah and threw him overboard, and the raging sea grew calm. At this the men greatly feared the Lord, and they offered a sacrifice to the Lord and made vows to him.*

The ship's crew did all they could to escape the storm's fury. They jettisoned their cargo, prayed, drew lots, rowed for the shore and, at last, when no other option remained, they threw Jonah overboard and cried out to the Lord for mercy.

God is never tied to a single agenda. He appears to be at work in one person and is involved with every other aspect of the situation too. The one who upholds the universe, made and kept going by him, is present everywhere, aware of the circumstances of every living creature and the happenings on every cubic inch of the planet—and beyond. As well as warning the Ninevites and bringing change in Jonah's heart, God was watching the sailors too. He saved their lives by calming the sea and because they were now convinced of his power they surrendered their souls to him.

Jonah might never have known this part of the story. There was no reason why he should meet those mariners again—perhaps he felt ashamed of putting their lives in such jeopardy—but someone told him how the sailors had found God. In heaven, when we find out how God used snippets of conversation, odd incidents and seemingly fruitless relationships, we will be astonished. Mostly the growth of his kingdom remains a secret down on earth, but occasionally God lets us see.

The sailors made vows which they kept; God heard their simple prayer. Their conversion was permanent and genuine. But it had not come about because Jonah was such a brilliant man of God. Even when we are faithless, he is faithful and is able to reveal himself so powerfully.

---

*Dear God, be good to me. The sea is so wide, and my boat is so small.*

OLD BRETON FISHERMAN'S PRAYER

CB

# The sign of the fish

*But the Lord provided a great fish to swallow Jonah, and Jonah was inside the fish three days and three nights.*

What went through Jonah's mind as he fell from the comparative safety of the stricken vessel into the raging sea? He must have expected to drown and maybe that's what he wanted: he was quite a depressive character and life had become impossible. At least his death would save the ship. The Lord had other plans, however, and as the waters closed over Jonah's head a giant fish swam up and swallowed him. When he regained consciousness, he was in the dark—in more ways than one. Why did God keep Jonah locked up in this living death for three days and nights? What came out of it?

God knew that only inside the fish would Jonah learn the lessons he needed to understand. Sometimes we find ourselves trapped where it is uncomfortable, frightening and dark. Your fish-belly may be an unhappy home, a disabling illness, or a hated job, and you feel that God has let you down and abandoned you. It is not easy to trust him to work everything together for good in it.

Jonah's ordeal had an effect far beyond his own life. His preaching to Nineveh meant thousands of lives were saved. Greater still was the sign he became centuries later when Jesus compared Jonah to himself. 'For as Jonah was three days and three nights in the belly of a huge fish, so the Son of Man will be three days and three nights in the heart of the earth' (Matthew 12:40). Christ gave up his life to save others and lay entombed until God raised him again. In our fallen world, some things can only be resolved through the suffering of God's servants, treasures painfully mined in the darkness. But he promises never to leave us.

---

*Christ leads me through*
*no darker rooms*
*Than he went through before;*
*He that unto*
*God's kingdom comes*
*Must enter by this door.*
RICHARD BAXTER (1615–91)

CB

# Jonah's prayer

*'When my life was ebbing away, I remembered you, Lord, and my prayer rose to you, to your holy temple... But I, with a song of thanksgiving, will sacrifice to you. What I have vowed I will make good. Salvation comes from the Lord.'*

Eventually Jonah started praying. It was as if this was what God was waiting for, because afterwards the fish was commanded to release Jonah. When we are very upset, angry or confused, it can be very hard to pray and sometimes it is the last thing we do. Better to swallow our pride—or our shame, whichever is causing us to avoid God's presence—and come early to the 'Father of compassion and the God of all comfort' (2 Corinthians 1:3) who longs to receive us as his children, humbly speaking words of confession, thanksgiving and pleas for help.

Jonah's prayer echoed the Psalms; he would have been very familiar with them from childhood and had learnt the importance of using scripture as he spoke to God. He expressed how he felt about what God had allowed to happen and 'called for help... from the depths of the grave'. Sometimes we wander round the mulberry bush instead of directly asking for what we need. Children can be like this, dropping hints and suggestions without ever coming out with what they are really after. This is frustrating, especially when you are fully aware of their agenda. Just ask!—with faith and thanksgiving.

The poignant beauty of chapter 2 is shown in how Jonah expresses his trust and hope in God. He is in danger but believes the Lord is going to pull him out. Resentment and fear gone, Jonah recommits himself to serving God, knowing that otherwise his existence is empty, pointless and perilous. And God hears and answers him.

---

*Jesus Christ, King of glory, help us to make the right use of all the myrrh that God sends, and to offer up the true incense of our hearts. Amen.*

LUKE JOHANN TAULER (1300–61)

CB

# Nineveh—the wicked city

*Jonah obeyed the word of the Lord and went to Nineveh. Now Nineveh was a very important city—a visit required three days. On the first day, Jonah started into the city. He proclaimed: 'Forty more days and Nineveh will be overturned.'*

Assyria was Israel's enemy, hated and resented. Nineveh was a huge metropolis, famed for its architecture, learning, culture—and sin. Jonah was rather like a man walking down London's Oxford Street wearing sandwich boards with 'Repent, the end is nigh!' written on them. Amazingly, nobody lynched him—he must have been fearful tramping through the streets, but perhaps, after all he had been through, he was resigned to whatever fate God had in store for him. Even more amazingly, he was not ignored, as most city street evangelists are. This week I have been praying for a 'Jews for Jesus' team working in London. It was great to hear today that passers-by are far more open and accepting of the gospel than on previous occasions.

We need to pray for the cities of our world where the spirits of materialism, corruption, lust and selfishness often dominate, and not be overwhelmed by them. Most of the world's population today live in large towns and cities and although many enjoy a prosperous lifestyle, the majority eke out their existence on very little. In the developing world, thousands of abandoned street-children scrabble for food scraps, quickly learning to blot out their misery by substance abuse—financed by crime, prostitution or begging. The poorest people so need help, and yet the situation seems so desperate. But all over the world God has his people in place, preaching the gospel, feeding the hungry and loving the dispossessed. His eyes are upon every individual; he does not want a single one to be lost.

---

*O Lord, who looked out over Jerusalem and wept, you have compassion for today's cities too, and want us to pray for your kingdom to come within them. Amen.*

**CB**

# Miracles of repentance

*The king… issued a proclamation… 'Let everyone call urgently on God. Let them give up their evil ways and their violence. Who knows? God may yet relent and with compassion turn from his fierce anger so that we will not perish.'*

The Ninevites' response to Jonah was extraordinary. It was not a case of a few who believed in God bringing some of their neighbours to faith. It was more significant than a National Day of Prayer—like when King George VI called the British people to pray for the troops trapped at Dunkirk. Jonah's message sparked off a national revival touching everyone. The Bible says, 'They declared a fast and all of them, from the greatest to the least, put on sackcloth.' The king himself wholeheartedly joined this repentance and prayer, laying aside the symbols of his royal authority and splendour and falling to the ground before God. He urged everyone to go beyond outward religious signs and sincerely turn away from 'their evil ways and violence'.

Paul wrote, 'Pray for all people. As you make your requests, plead for God's mercy upon them, and give thanks. Pray this way for kings and all others who are in authority, so we can live in peace and quietness, in godliness and dignity' (1 Timothy 2:1–2, NLT). Our leaders need prayer, whether they admit it or not. God longs to move in their lives, and we believe he will do so in response to our praying. As we begin, God will entrust us with certain insights to make our intercession more effective. Sometimes he will ask us to go beyond prayer and take action —send a letter or visit an MP, for example. We do not need to understand all the issues to ask God to help the Prime Minister, Cabinet, Opposition leaders and the Queen in their service for the nation. And if not us, who? If not now, when?

---

*Father, please remind us to pray for our nation and our world, especially that those in authority will turn to you. Amen.*

**CB**

# Can a nation be changed?

*When God saw what they did and how they turned from their evil ways, he had compassion and did not bring upon them the destruction he had threatened.*

Twenty-five years ago, Lyndon and I visited 'The Church on the Way' in California for a prayer meeting. We had never seen anything like this before: the prayer time was led by the Holy Spirit but dominating the room was an OHP screen on which were written not the words of the songs but all kinds of information about national and state government issues affecting society, along with Bible verses relating to them. With facts, figures, names and actual situations before them, intercessors were able to shoot the arrows of their prayers straight to the target. One after another they stood, made specific requests to God and thanked him for his merciful promises. I have never forgotten that inspiring evening.

The pastor of this Pentecostal church had begun this venture after reading 2 Chronicles 7:14: 'If my people, who are called by my name, will humble themselves and pray and seek my face and turn from their wicked ways, then will I hear from heaven and will forgive their sin and heal their land.' The prayer meeting was transformed by this scripture and it always began at 7.14 pm as a reminder to the congregation.

Our God is there, caring passionately about people. When the need for judgment is removed, he gladly turns aside from what he had planned. Never compromising, the Lord is ready to pour mercy and love through every crack he finds in the world's hard shell of sin. Nothing is impossible with him: nations and cities, kings and peasants can change if they are prepared to humble themselves before him.

---

*God is sheer mercy and grace; not easily angered, he's rich in love. He doesn't endlessly nag and scold, nor hold his grudges for ever. He doesn't treat us as our sins deserve, nor pay us back in full for our wrongs.*
PSALM 103:8–10, THE MESSAGE

CB

# Jonah's indignation

*But Jonah was greatly displeased and became angry. He prayed to the Lord, 'O Lord, is this not what I said when I was still at home? That is why I was so quick to flee to Tarshish. I knew that you are a gracious and compassionate God, slow to anger and abounding in love.'*

Can you credit it? After all Jonah had gone through and despite the extraordinary miracles he had personally experienced, when God told him that Nineveh was to be spared, he flew into a temper and wished he was dead. Why the violent reaction? You'd think he'd be thrilled to see God at work, using him, Jonah, and teaching him so much along the way. What was his problem?

Perhaps he felt his reputation was at stake. He had preached all over the city about its destruction and now nothing had happened. Is our desire to look good sometimes stronger than our longing for God's highest will to be accomplished? Do we mind not getting the credit, or looking out of place as a Christian in the company of non-believers? Stronger still was Jonah's deep-rooted hatred for the Assyrians—a little like the antipathy between the Jews and Gentiles in Christ's day, making it so hard for Peter to accept God's call to him to preach to the Gentiles. Do we care whether people in countries we dislike come to know the Lord? Men and women in prisons, illegal immigrants who compel their women and children to beg in our streets, those found guilty of child abuse... might a small part of us privately feel they are undeserving of salvation and love?

Facing our own meanness compared to God's never-ending grace is not easy. Jonah sat back and sulked, hoping against hope that the thunderbolts would crash down after all. But they didn't!

---

*For sin will have no dominion over you, since you are not under law but under grace.*
ROMANS 6:14 (NRSV)

CB

# Telling it as it was

*'Now, O Lord, take away my life, for it is better for me to die than to live.' But the Lord replied, 'Have you any right to be angry?'*

By now, our view of Jonah is tarnished, but don't forget that he wrote the book himself or else gave the details to someone else. How easily Jonah could have 'put a spin' on his story, presenting himself as a mature man of God, but we see what he was really like—disobedient, moody, cowardly and uncaring. By the end—and we have not reached it yet—he has learnt enough to be willing to present himself in a bad light, giving all the credit to God.

The events of Jonah cannot have taken long to unfold but in that short time the prophet went through a massive learning curve. God grants unique insights during difficult times, although this only happens when our hearts are right before him. I know a woman who has experienced great upheaval over the last eighteen months, facing her husband's unemployment, living in many temporary accommodations, coping with her child changing schools several times and caring for a dying parent. From time to time she phones and updates me, sharing her feelings of confusion and tiredness, but she never speaks with bitterness, and believes God is at work in their lives. Another acquaintance with a comparable story to tell never stops complaining and constantly accuses God of dealing unfairly with her.

It is a wonderful relief to be honest before God, confessing our true feelings towards him and holding on to what we believe about his character and ways. Even if we fail, as Jonah did, to respond graciously during our pain, let's share openly and with thankfulness and praise to God afterwards.

---

*A gentle Father and the God of all consolation, who comforts us in all our sorrows, so that we can offer others, in their sorrows, the consolation that we have received from God ourselves.*

2 CORINTHIANS 1:3–4 (JB)

**CB**

# Where do I shelter?

*Then the Lord God provided a vine and made it grow up over Jonah to give shade for his head to ease his discomfort, and Jonah was very happy about the vine. But at dawn the next day, God provided a worm, which chewed the vine so it withered.*

Jonah now sits in the blazing heat, still hoping. He does not want to know about God's all-embracing compassion for this hateful city and refuses to speak to him. Instead of finding shelter in God, he constructs something himself to block out the heat and wind.

We all try to anaesthetize ourselves from pain sometimes. It is very human to seek comfort in an effort to distract our minds from reality—for example, by over-indulging in food and drink, or making other things the focus and love of our lives, instead of running to God, our strength and hiding-place. He understands. Jesus is our 'high priest who is able to sympathize with our weaknesses, one who was tempted in every way, just as we are—yet was without sin' (Hebrews 4:15). When we turn away, he does not abandon us. Jonah notices that a large shady plant has miraculously appeared, which cheers him up enormously. In the same way, the Lord provides for us when we least deserve it.

Sometimes God is revealing that nothing compares with knowing him. Poor Jonah wakes up in the morning to find his vine dead and an unbearably hot wind whipping desert sands into his face. 'That's it! I am so angry with God, I want to die!' But God longs to show Jonah that the comfort he had found was fleeting and unreliable compared to the shelter of his great love.

---

*Everything I hope for comes from him, he's solid rock under my feet, breathing room for my soul, an impregnable castle. My help and glory are in God—so trust him absolutely, people; God is a safe place to be.*

Psalm 62:5–8 (The Message)

CB

# Grace to the city

*'You have been concerned about this vine, though you did not tend it or make it grow… But Nineveh has more than a hundred and twenty thousand people who cannot tell their right hand from their left, and many cattle as well. Should I not be concerned about that great city?'*

A small coin held up to the eye can obliterate the sun from sight. In the same way, we can allow insignificant preoccupations to cut us off from the light of God. Jonah's concerns had become so selfish that a withering wild desert plant, here today and gone tomorrow, had become far more important than the fate of a city full of people. His religious narrow-mindedness and bigotry made him uncaring about their dying without ever knowing God's salvation. There is nothing greater than God's love; Christ's death is the most significant moment in history, and yet most people dismiss it as unimportant or a myth. God longs for everyone of every generation to be saved. He knew that the city would be utterly destroyed at a later date, even though the Ninevites of Jonah's time repented. His heart was towards those individuals, regardless of their association with a city renowned for its wickedness over many years.

God also cared about the animals, the ecology of that region, for after all he is the creator and sustainer of the universe.

The book of Jonah was not very acceptable to some Jews, as it demonstrated God's grace and mercy far beyond them as a people, embracing the Gentile nations too. It shows us God's tender heart and patience, both towards troublesome Jonah and those outside his kingdom. His grace and loving kindness shine throughout the book into our lives as we read it.

---

*Dear Jesus, I don't want to be so taken up with other concerns that I no longer see your love present everywhere around us. Thank you for your mercy and grace. I want always to follow wherever you lead. Amen.*

**CB**

# Promises to the crowds

*But the angel said to them, 'Do not be afraid. I bring you good news of great joy that will be for all the people. Today in the town of David a Saviour has been born to you: he is Christ the Lord... Glory to God in the highest, and on earth peace to men on whom his favour rests.'*

Familiar words. It's almost impossible to separate them from the aroma of roasting turkey, the rustle of presents, or the unforgettable atmosphere of a church lit and decorated for Christmas.

However, when these words were first spoken, no one had yet thought of Christmas. Did the angels know they would be quoted so often? This glorious moment when heaven broke through to announce the new order was nothing to do with red and green candles. This was a message of freedom, declared to everyone. This affirmation was for the whole of humankind. Hey people, God likes you! He is sending his Son who will save you! Isn't that the best news ever? There will be joy and peace for everyone! Then the angels burst with excitement into sky-blazing praise of God.

Joy, peace, salvation, favour, God's glory—what a mandate. God promised all this through Jesus. As Jesus began his public ministry some thirty years later, were there any in the gathering crowds who remembered these promises? As we take a few days to join the crowds, bear in mind these clear promises of God. The people who gathered to Jesus could look for the good stuff, for real good news. There would be no need for anyone to feel reticent or ignored. This great joy was for *all* people. Every person who came to hear what this new Rabbi was saying had the same opportunity. The good and great promises of God, fulfilled in this man, offered to you.

---

*Ever feel just one of a crowd? Jesus does not see you that way. No one is left out in 'all'.*

*Read Luke 4:14–21. Jesus knew what he had come for.*

**DA**

# The crowds begin

*Jesus went through all the towns and villages, teaching in their synagogues, preaching the good news of the kingdom and healing every disease and sickness.*

It really is not surprising that Jesus attracted crowds. Can you imagine yourself among them? There were other itinerant rabbis of course. But the word was out that Jesus of Nazareth was different. For a start, he had this amazing authority that made you want to listen for more (Matthew 7:29). He was not afraid of opponents and had a cavalier attitude to the laws which ordinary folk struggled to keep. Why, one Sabbath he dramatically healed a woman during his own teaching slot. Then he took to task those who criticized him for 'working' on the Sabbath. It was the talk of the town and the crowd was delighted with the wonderful drama. The healings, well, they had to be seen to be believed. It was astonishing to watch him make people better. It made you ask the question—who is he? (Matthew 12: 23). Somehow he made you feel closer to God and want to praise him for the wonderful things you were seeing and hearing (Luke 18:43).

Small wonder, then, that the crowds grew. The question is, if you had been there, would you have joined them? Would you have left your housework and rushed to hear him when he came to town? Or would you have been too busy? Would you have grabbed a sick friend's hand and hurried through the dusty streets, hope rising as you saw a space at the front of the crowd? Or would you have dallied alone at the back, in case nothing happened? Would you have listened attentively to his surprising stories, wrestled with the difficult bits, but come back for more? Or would your mind have wandered to the prospects for next market day?

---

*Then, as now, we are so human, with so many mixed motives. What do you come to Jesus for, and do you trust him to be there for you?*

**DA**

# The crowds persist

*At daybreak Jesus went out to a solitary place. The people were looking for him and when they came to where he was, they tried to keep him from leaving them. But he said, 'I must preach the good news of the kingdom of God to the other towns also, because that is why I was sent.'*

Once people got a taste for all Jesus was offering, they wanted more. They chased after him when he looked for some space, and hung on to him when he wanted to leave. Most of them were wonderfully ordinary folk. Certainly the teachers and Pharisees joined in, as the stir Jesus created demanded their attention. The powerful people were there. But the majority were the ordinary folk of Galilee, mesmerized by a teacher they could understand and respond to.

Jesus did not call the Jewish religious leaders together to proclaim his mission and ask for their endorsement. He patently did not use the social, political or religious structures of the day to give his message clout. He never responded to the seductive trappings of power.

Given the questionable security of human power structures, this is good news. Jesus stood alone, not dependent on any human institution. He was exclu-sively obedient to his Father in heaven. He shared the good news of the kingdom with everyday people and excluded no one who wanted to listen. He was honest about the demands of the kingdom, but only the religious leaders earned his explicit condemnation (Matthew 23)—an awesome challenge for those with similar responsibilities today.

He chose his disciples from among the ordinary Jews. He was particularly close to Peter, James and John. He was the son of God walking the hills of Judah, but he was normal. His friends were normal. He invites us, as ordinary humans, to be his friends today.

---

*Dear Lord Jesus, some days I feel ordinary, some days I feel great, and some days I feel distinctly weird. Thank you that you invite me to be your friend every day. Amen.*

*Read John 15:15–16.*

DA

# Jesus' attitude

*When he saw the crowds, he had compassion on them, because they were harassed and helpless, like sheep without a shepherd.*

Jesus' attitude to the multitudes that surrounded him was consistent. He had compassion. He had compassion when they were hungry, and the miracle of the feeding of the five thousand ensued. He had compassion when they were ill, and healed them. He told a riveting story about a compassionate father who ran to embrace his prodigal son, and set the scene for many of us to return to our heavenly Father in the same way. Jesus saw people's struggles, had compassion and acted in love. No wonder the crowds followed him.

There are some heartwarming accounts of individuals who stand out from the crowd. Many of them—oh yes!—were women. There was Peter's mother-in-law, healed of a fever, and Jairus' daughter, rescued from death. There was the oh-so-brave woman who touched the edge of Jesus' cloak. In touching him she broke levitical laws, as she was ceremonially unclean from her illness and a woman at that. But Jesus responded with compassion, acknowledging her healing and uniquely calling her 'Daughter'.

Each person was treated with the utmost dignity and compassion by Jesus. They must represent so many other encounters Jesus had which were not written down. So many discovered that Jesus really did bring good news, joy and peace. It is so encouraging that even when the people broke through cultural and religious boundaries to get to him, they all received the same treatment. I have a theory that it was the women who had more courage in this than the men. Think of the Canaanite woman, begging for her daughter's restoration (Mark 7:24–30), or the lady lavishing tears and perfume on Jesus' feet in the middle of a meal.

Each one refused to stay away. Each one received Jesus' compassion.

---

*Whether you feel near or far away from God today, do not let anything keep you from coming closer.*

**DA**

# Whisperings

*Among the crowds there was widespread whispering about him.
Some said, 'He is a good man.' Others replied, 'No, he deceives
the people.' But no one would say anything publicly about him
for fear of the Jews.*

Nothing new here. Nothing new about the way some people will respond readily to Jesus, while others will judge and condemn. It was fair enough that people should have asked searching questions as to Jesus' identity. They did not have the benefit of hindsight as we do. When we meet Jesus it can only be as the risen Christ, gloriously alive in the here and now. Then, the Jews had to struggle with explosive issues. Was he the Messiah, the Promised One? Did he really do these remarkable healings by the power of God? What did he mean when he claimed to be the bread of life? No separation of synagogue and state then, no question of Jesus being an irrelevance. If he was the Messiah, the political implications would be cataclysmic. Likewise if he was not.

These were enormous questions. Yet it seems Jesus was most able to respond to those who set all their agendas aside and simply came to him in honesty, need and openness. These were the ones who received his compassion. The others, the scribes and Pharisees who tried to catch him out with their cunning, rendered themselves blind to Jesus' true nature. They were so anxious about the political implications and so enmeshed in their religious structures that they could not relate. Were they cynical and hardhearted or just misguided? Perhaps both. But we all know people who seem incapable of enthusiasm for anything except their own point of view. They seem to have forgotten that good news, joy and peace really do exist. How could the ruling Jews not see the calibre of person Jesus was? Eventually they influenced even the crowds to betray Jesus and call for his death.

---

*Are you free to respond with open-hearted simplicity to Jesus? Treat yourself to some 'me-time' to do just that today.*

*Read Matthew 18:2–10.*

**DA**

# Doubt in the crowd

*Then the eleven disciples went to Galilee, to the mountain where Jesus had told them to go. When they saw him, they worshipped him; but some doubted. Then Jesus came to them and said, 'All authority in heaven and on earth has been given to me... And surely I am with you always, to the very end of the age.'*

I find these words some of the most remarkable in the Bible. Did you spot them? That little phrase, 'but some doubted'. How on earth did they do that? These were the guys who had travelled the road with Jesus. They knew him so well. They had eaten food he provided out of nowhere. They had spoken to those he had healed. They had been empowered by the Holy Spirit to do the same. Then they had tumbled from excitement into terror as the forces ranging against this unpredictable, unownable teacher closed in. They ran when he was arrested and hid when he was crucified. They thought that was it. They would never see him again. Back, somehow, to tax collecting and fishing.

Then another emotional twister as he appeared to them in a risen body. Wow! Back on line again, but in a whole new dimension!

So how did they doubt? They saw what so many of us wished we had seen, and yet they doubted! How could they disbelieve even the evidence of their own eyes? Is it why God so often withholds himself from us today when we are begging for a sign? Is this why he does not reveal himself clearly to the world in general? Perhaps it would not make any difference.

*The miracles did just what Jesus had predicted. To those who chose to believe him, they gave even more reason to believe. But for those determined to deny him, the miracles made little difference. Some things just have to be believed to be seen.*

Philip Yancey, *Disappointment with God* (Marshall Pickering, 1995)

---

*Dear Father, have mercy on us. We want to see, and worship. Amen.*

DA

# The crowds leave

*From this time many of his disciples turned back and no longer followed him. 'You do not want to leave too, do you?' Jesus asked the Twelve. Simon Peter answered him, 'Lord, to whom shall we go? You have the words of eternal life.'*

If yesterday's verses included one of my most puzzling phrases, today's contain one of my favourite. When life seems at its bleakest and faith at its lowest, there is always that indisputable awareness that Jesus is it. There is nowhere else to go, no one else to turn to. No one else offers words of eternal life. I guess different scriptures grab different people but I have returned countless times to Peter's words and found in them the steadying security I need.

Yet the occasion which prompted Peter's declaration must have been such a sad one for Jesus. His ministry had attracted all those wonderful, excitable, enthusiastic crowds, eager to receive his compassion. But as soon as Jesus began to say truths they did not want to hear, their commitment fell away. This must have been much harder for Jesus than facing up to his enemies in the crowds. Opponents are one thing, but friends who desert are another. Though he never wavered, or watered down his message, it must have been heartbreaking for Jesus to see his friends unable to digest the bread of life he was giving them.

The parallels are obvious. Do we stay the course when the terrain gets rough? Do we too try to take the bits of Jesus we like and leave the rest? Are we determined to stick by Jesus because we know his are the words of eternal life, no matter how unpalatable?

I imagine that those who turned away returned to their lives in disillusionment. Perhaps they criticized Jesus robustly to ease their emptiness. Perhaps they were quiet and sad. Surely many must have wondered why life was never quite the same again.

---

*Dear Father, I worship and praise you for Jesus. How could anything compare to him? Amen.*

*Read Revelation 7:9–17.*

**DA**

# The anchor of hope

*We who have taken refuge might be strongly encouraged to seize the hope set before us. We have this hope, a sure and steadfast anchor of the soul.*

'I went to a Christian's funeral last year, and they were all happy saying Karen was in a better place. I looked around and thought, "Am I the only one here who is angry that she's died and left three little children without a mother?"' I shifted gear as a casual conversation over sausage rolls at a party suddenly demanded a response that would embrace the pain and bewilderment that this acquaintance had expressed. It was tough.

She had articulated a profound truth: death brings earthly relationships to a cruel end, and it is wrong not to acknowledge the tragedy. Yet there is something else that as a non-believer she could only observe rather than experience—hope is inseparable from faith in God.

Hope does not deny the presence of evil and suffering. We may often feel like frail little boats in a storm, tossed by the waves, beaten by the wind and deafened by the roar of the gale. Terrified, we may think we're about to drown. Yet as the writer to the Hebrews reminds us, as

Christians, we have a sure and steadfast anchor of the soul which we must seize, which penetrates deep into the invisible world beneath the storm. This anchor is the hope we have through faith in Christ.

Hebrews was written to Christians who were weather-beaten by persecution and spiritual doubt. It encourages them and us not to give up, with reminders of unchanging eternal truths which though hidden, are utterly real.

The English Protestant martyr and bishop, John Hooper, the night before he was executed for his faith in 1555, wrote: *'Let nothing cause thy heart to fail; launch out thy boat, hoist up thy sail, put from the shore; and be sure thou shalt attain unto the port that shall remain for evermore.'*

This man had a hope, anchored in Christ, that could see beyond death.

---

*Now faith is the assurance of things hoped for, the conviction of things not seen (Hebrews 11:1).*

**FB**

# Hope's companions

*We want each one of you to show the same diligence so as to realize the full assurance of hope to the very end.*

I would love walking on mountains if they weren't so steep. My lack of fitness leaves me panting, and I'm even rendered speechless which is a severe trial (if only to me). Despite all these objections, I keep finding myself at the foot of great peaks, rucksack on my back, hiking boots on my feet, and that sinking feeling in my stomach. Amazingly, although I'm inevitably last, I do reach the summit.

What gets me up there? Well, there's the promise of a spectacular view at the top. I believe those who say the climb is worth it, and past experience of other scenes feeds that hope. But there's something else that keeps me going, and that is love. You see, my friends have noted my enfeebled state, so that their coaxing and Mars bars spur me on to scale the heights with them.

The Hebrew Christians were finding the climb too hard. Their limbs were tired and sore. The only realities seemed to be the hard stones of opposition and the endless path before them with no sign of relief.

The writer warns of the dire consequences of abandoning their walk, but also assures them of unseen and unchanging eternal truths. The three legged stool of faith, hope and love is there for them to rest on as they persevere up the mountain. They must keep in mind the breath-taking, magnificent end which is the hope fed by faith. And so that they do not become selfish in their journey, they are encouraged to care for others.

'Love! Hope! Have faith!' are the instructions to them and also to those who identify with their weariness. In Hebrews 11, we are joined by a vast array of climbers, whose potted biographies help us to enter into the experience of faith and hope and love of believers who persevered.

*Help me, Lord, to keep on keeping on. Amen.*

FB

# Stories of hope

*Now faith is the assurance of things hoped for, the conviction
of things not seen.*

Since cradle days, thousands of sermons have been directed my way, so by now, I know more or less what I'm supposed to do as a Christian. When things go wrong, it is not so much on account of ignorance, but discouragement, laziness, loss of motivation or plain disobedience. It can also be lack of vision: I'm so preoccupied with what's going on around me that I fail to look up. I don't see the big picture. I lose hope.

If all else fails, there are two activities which inspire me to think beyond my troubles and continue the hard path of commitment. The first is watching other people—and I learn as much from their mistakes as from their 'successes'. The second is listening to stories, which become like pictures in my thinking to help me understand.

I am not alone in being drawn to chapter 11 out of all the chapters in Hebrews, precisely because here all the theology, the warnings and the encouragement to persevere are given flesh and bones in the stories of individuals. They lived at different times, and in various places; their experiences and personalities were many. However, the common factor was that at their core they were people of faith fed by hope.

In this introduction, the writer gives a definition of faith which shows its close relationship to hope: 'Now faith is the assurance of things hoped for, the conviction of things not seen.' In other words, the reality of what we hope for is confirmed for us in our experience when we live by faith in God's promises. Or, as Peter Anderson has stated, 'Hope is faith in the future tense' (*Gathered Gold*, ed. John Blanchard, Evangelical Press, 1984).

So let us listen to these stories and learn from these people. The faith they demonstrated may teach us to recognize and value the hope which was theirs, so we may imitate them.

---

*Teach me, Lord, to expect in hope
what I believe in faith.*

**FB**

# Hopeful worship

*By faith Abel offered to God a more acceptable*
*sacrifice than Cain's.*

I've always found it rather strange when people seek to emphasize just how close they are to a particular friend by saying, 'We're just like sisters/brothers'. When I do a random internal roll call of siblings I have known, such intimacy is not the first thing that springs to mind. Brothers and sisters may file in together to a pew on Sunday, smile forbearingly for family photos and even stick up for each other in the playground. However, much of the time the relationship is one of rivalry, competition and jealousy.

The story of brothers Cain and Abel raises many questions. Had there always been tension between them? Is that why they worked apart, one as a shepherd and the other tilling the ground? What did their parents tell them about how God was to be approached? Why did God accept the offering Abel made and reject that brought by Cain? Neither Genesis 4 nor Hebrews gives explanations, though there are some clues. Genesis states that Abel brought God the fat portions of his flock's firstlings, the very best. He recognized that God's utter worthiness had to be reflected in the worship he offered. Importantly, it was his attitude that earned God's approval. Abel was righteous, while Cain's subsequent rage and murder reveal a different outlook.

These two brothers came from the same parents, may have looked alike and presumably had a similar upbringing. To the casual observer, both brought equivalent gifts to God, namely produce from their daily labour. Yet only God was able to see deep into their hearts. Only God could recognize where there was confident hope in him. For worship has God, rather than self, as its focus. Indeed, it came from a faith which cost Abel his life.

In our own age when appearance and image is so important, both within and outside the church, Abel's faith still speaks.

---

*How can I be sure that the worship I bring is acceptable to God?*
**FB**

# Salvation hope

*By faith Noah, warned by God about events as yet unseen, respected the warning and built an ark to save his household.*

How do you convince people that you have a relationship with God, and yet are still normal? How do you explain that you talk to him in prayer and he speaks to you through his word without sounding like a complete nutter? This is my struggle, because I long to introduce people to Jesus, but don't want to be dismissed along with those who converse with fairies and extra-terrestrials.

Noah was not reluctant to look odd. Living in an evil and depraved society, he stood out because he 'was a righteous man... Noah walked with God' (Genesis 6:9).

There was more. Unaffected by the fear of mockery, Noah began to build a boat on dry land. There was no sign of rain, nor was it usual to put the local wildlife into confined spaces. The man was barking mad!

Yet in God's eyes, and in view of the subsequent flood, he was the sanest man on earth. He walked with God, so was privy to his thoughts. This wasn't just a new hobby; he single-mindedly allowed God's warning of judg-ment on evil and the promise of salvation to shape his whole life. The Lord's heart must have been so warmed by Noah's faith and his unshakeable hope despite intolerable circumstances and neighbours. Indeed, he was the sign to his contemporaries of God's promised future, the focus of hope for a new start.

At times we may well be dismissed as crazy. We'll be in good company—and it's OK, as long as we are also blameless, righteous and walking with God. As Christians, we do have an understanding of future events, namely that Jesus will return again as Saviour and Judge. It would be disloyal to God, irresponsible to those who need to hear his word of warning and hope, and indeed sheer madness, to pretend we didn't.

---

*Thank you, Jesus, for being my Saviour. Help me to prepare others for your return.*

                                              FB

# Hope for the hopeless

*By faith he (Abraham) received power of procreation, even
though he was too old—and Sarah herself was barren—because
he considered him faithful who had promised.*

Childlessness was a painful
enough aspect in the life of
Abraham and Sarah without
God having to draw attention to
it. Even by the time God called
them from Haran to go to
Canaan, Abraham at 75 years
old would have resigned himself
to never becoming a father. Yet
it was then that the Lord began
to refer to his descendants.
There must have been a strange
sort of cocktail of despair and
hope in his heart every time
God repeated the promise of a
child without giving a date.

It's worth noting that these
two verses in Hebrews sum-
marise over twenty years of
waiting in hope. And while
Abraham did trust in God's
promise, the account in Genesis
12—20 also tells how at times
he and Sarah found the anguish
and disappointment unbearable.

Yet this hope was not just the
object of these senior citizens'
personal dreams. In God's
unsearchable plan, this child
was also the means by which
God's purpose for a nation,
indeed for the blessing of the

world, would be realized. That's
why God didn't give up even
when Abraham and Sarah,
through sheer emotional fatigue
were tempted to abandon 'hoping against hope' (Romans
4:18).

It's hard to comprehend why
God sometimes gives us longings
that threaten to overwhelm us,
with no hope of fulfilment. It's a
mystery why some prayers for
what we believe to be God's will
seem unanswered for years.
Abraham and Sarah would
understand. They also know
that eventually their tears were
turned to laughter as the Lord
miraculously chose to give life
where there appeared to be no
hope. Our God can bring life to
dead things, even after it seems
to be 'too late'.

---

*God of the impossible, give me
faith and patience to trust you
even when my heart is breaking.*
                              **FB**

# Deliverance hope

*By faith Moses was hidden by his parents for three months after his birth, because they saw that the child was beautiful; and they were not afraid of the king's edict.*

On her mantelpiece, my friend Janette had three cards with little photos of infants being carried by storks. 'Each baby looks exactly the same,' I declared, stating what I believed to be the obvious. 'Perhaps these photographers have one shot which they use for every birth announcement.' Janette was not amused.

For parents, especially, their child is unique. Although now it is only a scrunched up piece of noise and smell, they see unmistakeable signs of it being a great beauty or a genius.

Moses was born at a time when there was little reason for hope. Baby boys were under the king's death sentence, and for those who survived, there was no future other than a life of slavery and victimization. Would it not just have been easier for Moses' family to give up in despair?

Not at all. God used natural parental hope to effect an amazing deliverance, not only for this one baby, but for the whole people of Israel. By faith, Moses'

parents believed that their God was more powerful than Pharaoh.

It was this hope which led them to make the very practical arrangement of floating him in a basket on the Nile under the watchful eye of his sister. Their trust in God's deliverance was rewarded when, amazingly, Pharaoh's daughter became his human protector.

Anyone who cares for children has plenty of reasons to fear for their future. Yet while giving them love and protection and nourishment, we also have no choice but to let them go, not into a river, but into the hands of God. Our hopes for them can inform our prayers of faith. For Moses' parents, it involved a future for which they might never have dared to hope, beyond their wildest dreams.

---

*God of deliverance, teach me how to hold and how to release those you have entrusted to me. Amen.*

**FB**

# Imperishable hope

*By faith Moses, when he was grown up, refused to be called a son of Pharaoh's daughter, choosing rather to share ill-treatment with the people of God rather than to enjoy the fleeting pleasures of sin.*

Moses would have been a prime candidate for *Hello* magazine: 'King's grandson invites us to his apartments and speaks to us for the first time about life in the palace.' Any exclusive would be a scoop for editors and a 'must' for readers to drool over and envy.

Brought up in the palace after his own mother had nursed him, Moses had the best of everything. He would have been educated by the most able of tutors in the legendary wisdom of Egypt. His prospects were the brightest.

Then came a point of crisis, in Exodus 2, when Moses made a deliberate choice to identify not with the splendour of privilege, but with an insignificant band of slaves living in abject misery. He saw that there are more valuable things in life than material treasures and advantages. His royal lifestyle turned sour because he understood that it was sustained by exploitation and cruelty.

By faith, Moses set his hope on eternal spiritual rewards which he believed to be of much greater value than the physical wealth he possessed. He realized that he could not turn a blind eye on what was happening, and so chose to turn his back on the treasures of Egypt in order to identify with God's people.

In our own relatively affluent society which values money, education, success and ambition, it is sometimes hard to see where Christians are different. Providing for the family through hard work, taking time for leisure and social relationships are all important, but perhaps this radical example of Moses can serve to remind us that God's children are born to a new hope. Our goals have to be different.

---

*Read Titus 2:11–13 and Romans 8:18–21.*

**FB**

# Hope for the fearful

*By faith he (Moses) left Egypt, unafraid of the king's anger; for he persevered as though he saw him who is invisible.*

It has been said that courage is fear that has said its prayers. The first century Christians, amid persecution and hostility, needed their faith strengthened and enlarged. So they were reminded of Moses.

When mention is made of Moses leaving Egypt, the readers would recall that which preceded it. They would remember how Moses fled in fear to Midian when he killed a cruel Egyptian. They would know that God's call to deliver his people from slavery was met with many excuses from a panic-stricken Moses: he reckoned he didn't know who God was, he assumed the Israelites wouldn't believe God had sent him, he claimed that he was not eloquent and finally pleaded for someone else to be asked instead of him. 'To boldly go' was not his theme tune.

Yet Hebrews 11 claims he was 'unafraid' of the king's anger. Is this glossing over the story in Exodus 3—4?

Perhaps an answer lies in the fact that fear and courage are not incompatible. As Moses pleaded time and again with Pharaoh for the release of the Israelites, there is nothing to say that his knees weren't knocking. However, he had stopped the fear mastering and controlling him.

Pharaoh was a powerful figure, but Moses knew that God was Almighty. When God translated Moses' unarticulated hopes and frustration for his people into a call to action, he spoke from a bush burning with holiness. Moses' fear of God, as well as his confident expectation in him, grew as he was obedient.

God's call to proclaim his message to a hostile world, whether in the time of Moses, the first century or the twenty-first will give his people every reason to be afraid. Yet it is our hope in the utter faithfulness of God that makes us strong and enables us to persevere.

---

*Almighty God, please don't let my fears be an excuse for ignoring your call. Amen.*

**FB**

# Awe-filled hope

*By faith the people passed through the Red Sea as if it were dry land, but when the Egyptians attempted to do so they were drowned.*

'Our fear must save our hope from swelling into presumption, and our hope must save our fear from sinking into despair' (Matthew Henry, *Gathered Gold*, ed. John Blanchard, Evangelical Press, 1984). Hope is not invulnerable. It is neither tidy nor triumphant, but needs to be nurtured like a sensitive flower. Hebrews 11 includes the story of the crossing of the Red Sea to breathe faith and hope into Christians who were flagging.

Exodus 14 describes how the Israelites' boldness turned to despair as they became sandwiched between the advancing Egyptians and the sea. They cried out to Moses, 'Was it because there were no graves in Egypt that you have taken us away to die in the wilderness?' (Exodus 14:11). Too soon after expectations had soared, they plummeted.

All Moses could do was cry out to the Lord. This was just one of many incidents where hope in God was sustained in severe testing—and then in triumph, for the Lord 'turned the sea into dry land, and the waters were divided' (Exodus 14:21).

It must have taken considerable courage for the first person and then the rest to step forward with a wall of water on either side. Moses had challenged them to 'stand firm, and see the deliverance that the Lord will accomplish for you today' (Exodus 14:13). With the enemy at their heels, they had no choice but to hold on to this hope and go forward.

The Egyptians, however, had no sensitivities. Without stopping to wonder at this miracle of God, they followed the Israelites onto the sea bed. Their presumption met with God's judgment and they all drowned.

'Israel saw the great work that the Lord did against the Egyptians. So the people feared the Lord and believed in the Lord and in his servant Moses' (Exodus 14:31).

---

*Thank you, Lord, for the events you use to strengthen our hope in you. Keep in us a sense of awe, and never presumption. Amen.*

**FB**

# Hope based on experience

*And what more should I say?*
*For time would fail me to tell of… David.*

Several years ago, I was talking to someone who I'd always considered to be reasonably sane. He was telling me about a conference he'd attended: 'It was so good, because it helped you to discover problems you didn't even know you had.' I remember smiling meekly and deciding I'd certainly give that place a wide berth!

Most of us have enough troubles without having to scrape around for hidden difficulties. Sometimes it seems as though there is no end to the obstacles which trip us up and stop us from enjoying a peaceful and happy existence.

David was no stranger to problems and tragedy. The despised and forgotten younger brother may have been chosen by God as king, but the privilege involved considerable hardship. In the first instance, King Saul was intensely jealous, so David lived as a fugitive in fear of his life for years. Even after his coronation, he experienced repeated heartache as self-interested friends and family betrayed him. 1 and 2 Samuel and 1 Chronicles detail many personal and national struggles.

The Psalms too reveal something of David's inner life during times of turmoil. The most recurring theme is his trust in the Lord to whom he poured out his heart. Again and again as he saw earthly and human security crumble around him, he recognized that God alone was his hope.

What was the ground of David's faith? It was his personal experience of God's presence in his life. When as an insignificant lad he faced the mighty giant Goliath, he did not doubt God's strength, because he had proved it with lions and bears as he guarded his father's sheep. The situations which faced him after Goliath were often of gigantic proportions, yet these were opportunities to call on God and experience his presence and salvation—again and again.

---

*I will sing to the Lord, because he has dealt bountifully with me (Psalm 13:6).*

**FB**

# Hope to guide

*And what more should I say?*
*For time would fail me to tell of... Samuel.*

An agnostic schoolboy was set an essay on euthanasia. He remembers making the point that he couldn't see why all Christians didn't commit suicide immediately: after all, if heaven promised to be such a wonderful place, why wait before tucking into the blessings?

Nowadays, as a Christian himself, he sees things differently, for knowing God gives us hope in this world as well as for the next. This hope motivates our worship and daily living. We realize that we have to give an account of our attitudes and behaviour on this earth; out of love for Jesus, we long to be rewarded with his 'Well done!'

It was this hope which kept Samuel faithful to God's word from childhood as a dogsbody in the temple until his death in old age. The historic link between the era of the judges and the monarchy, his principal role was as a prophet, listening to God and bringing his message to Israel. Such honour brought repeated discouragement as the people and then King Saul chose to ignore his warnings and teachings.

In 1 Samuel 12, as he presents Israel with the human king they should never have demanded, Samuel puts aside disappointment and personal rejection. He begs them to serve the Lord the King wholeheartedly and to go his way. He repeats his entreaty that they reflect something of the goodness of their God in their everyday behaviour. He cannot cease praying for them to that effect. And why? 'For the Lord will not cast away his people, for his great name's sake, because it has pleased the Lord to make you a people for himself' (v. 22).

---

*Thank you, Lord, for the hope we have knowing that you have chosen us for Yourself. Help us to reflect this in our worship and our daily lives.*

**FB**

# Hope that influences

*And what more should I say?*
*For time would fail me to tell of... the prophets.*

*He has told you, O mortal, what is good; and what does the Lord*
*require of you but to do justice, and to love kindness, and to walk*
*humbly with your God?*

Going shopping increasingly forces me to juggle between my conscience and my purse. The great love I have for bargains often seems at loggerheads with ethical values. Major coffee and tea companies may lure me with tempting offers, but can I be sure that those who picked the beans and leaves were given a fair wage? Some clothes and cuddly toys may seem surprisingly cheap, but is it costing workers in sweat factories their health and family life? It is an exceedingly complicated moral and international business maze, but I am not free to ignore my responsibility to the exploited.

Many named and unnamed prophets were sent to God's people to remind them of just such issues. Through picture language and sermon, symbolic action and writing, they condemned 'faith' that was only a private affair or a national ritual; it had to be evidenced in the very fabric of everyday social behaviour. Prophets voiced God's warnings of judgment on sin. They were often ignored and snubbed, persecuted and ridiculed.

'The Christian hope is not a matter of tickling our minds but for changing our lives and for influencing society' (Stephen Travis, *Gathered Gold*). God's ultimate will for the future is a kingdom of justice and peace, love and compassion, equality and respect. If we as God's people have such hopes, should we not be working towards that now? Should we not be demonstrating God's concern for the oppressed and despairing—at the very least in our shopping baskets?

---

*Is this not the fast that I choose:*
*to loose the bonds of injustice...*
*to let the oppressed go free...? Is*
*it not to share your bread with*
*the hungry, and bring the home-*
*less poor into your house; when*
*you see the naked, to cover them?*
Isaiah 58:6–7

**FB**

# Kingdom hope

*Therefore, since we are surrounded by so great a cloud of witnesses, let us also lay aside every weight and the sin that clings so closely, and let us run with perseverance the race that is set before us, looking to Jesus.*

When Jesus began his public ministry, he announced that 'the kingdom of God is near'. In the three years which followed, he illustrated in his teaching and his miracles just what the kingdom would be like—one of love and justice, peace and truth, healing and wholeness. His resurrection confirmed the promise that God's reign would be established eternally. And yet we, like the Hebrew believers, are often more aware of the God-rejecting kingdom of darkness.

So in encouraging us to consider Jesus' endurance, the writer also reminds us that now he is seated at the right hand of the throne of God. His work is complete. He is king.

For his followers, however, the task is not finished. We need to be visual representations of God's reign in our attitudes and behaviour. We are required to demonstrate and promote kingdom values. We cannot give up. Together as God's people, we must act as an arrow pointing to God's future.

Trust in God's sovereignty is the basis for our hope. In this life we are guaranteed trouble, yet one day, Jesus will return to put an end to all evil. Then we have the wonderful promise of eternal life, a new creation and the full revelation of the glory of God.

What will the future bring? Will natural or technological disaster bring an end to the world? While we may have no answers to these questions, as Christians we have one certain hope: Jesus is King, and one day no one, not even the devil himself, will be in any doubt.

---

*Sovereign Lord, reign in my life until your kingdom comes in all its fullness. Amen.*

**FB**

# 1 Corinthians

First-century Corinth was the original 'Seaside Sin City'. Think Rio de Janeiro or San Francisco: anything goes, every day, every night. The Greeks had a word for it: a life of debauchery was to *Korinthiaszein*—to live like a Corinthian.

Corinth stands on a narrow isthmus, four miles wide, linking southern Greece with the north. Anybody going north, south, east or west had to go through Corinth. This bottleneck effect made the city chaotic, hustling, and prosperous.

Scholars have described first-century Corinth as the 'most populated, wealthy, commercially-minded and sex-obsessed city of eastern Europe'. Its 250,000 inhabitants included Roman bourgeois and ex-soldiers, Greek philosophers and adventurers, Phoenician sailors, Jewish entrepreneurs, and every sort of merchant, freedman, slave, and huckster.

Towering over the city was the Acrocorinth—a high hill with a huge temple to Aphrodite, the Greek goddess of love. Her 1000 priestesses were temple prostitutes, and worked the city each night. Then there was the Temple of Apollo—god of music, song and poetry; also, the ideal of male beauty. Boys were its temple prostitutes, making Corinth a centre of homosexual practices.

Paul reached the city about March of AD50. This frenzied urban hotchpotch was the biggest city he had ever seen—no wonder Paul talked of 'fear and trembling' on his arrival. Corinth was enough to awe anyone—and to survey the city with the idea of preaching about Jesus Christ was mind-boggling. The forces arrayed against Paul were great, and he was alone, frail, and not in the best of health.

Paul's 18-month stay in Corinth is recorded in Acts 18: 1–18. He worked as a tent-maker and taught in his spare time, until people were willing to support him as a loved teacher.

Scholars believe Paul stayed until about September AD51. Then he moved on. But he kept in touch by letter. Scholars date 1 Corinthians as very late AD53 or early 54.

Corinth faced many of the same problems as our modern-day cities. This letter was written to meet those needs and is as relevant today as it was then.

*Anne Coomes*

# You were called

*Paul, called... by the will of God... to the church of God... called to be holy.*

Why are you a Christian? Because you decided to be? Yes, but what made you even consider it in the first place? Because *God called you*, and you said yes.

God's calling to us as individuals is vital to Paul's thinking. If you have time today, read the entire first chapter and count up the times he uses variations of call–called–calling.

Clearly this sense of God calling each one of us is at the front of Paul's mind as he begins this letter to the church he had founded at Corinth. It gave him a much-needed divine perspective on the Corinthian Christians, because they were far from 'saintly' in their actions!

From Paul's letter, we find they were class-conscious, sexually permissive, vague on doctrine, resentful of anyone telling them what to do, and quick to take offence with each other. They resisted the Holy Spirit's daily efforts to transform their lives with love and humility, but they wanted him to enliven their worship services with lots of dramatic happenings.

That was the Corinthian church then, and sadly it sounds like many churches today.

But God didn't give up on them, and he doesn't give up on churches today, and he doesn't give up on us as individuals.

Are things spiritually dry in your life at present? Do you wonder where all the joy and spiritual power is that some Christians seem to find? Go back to the beginning, as Paul does here. Go back to your beginning with God. Think again as to why you are a Christian in the first place. Because God called you. Remember that moment when, deep in your inner self, you glimpsed something of the love of God *for you*... and you responded.

Savour your conversion for what it was... it was God seeking you. You were called. There is still time to live up to your calling. Because God is still calling you.

---

*Read John 15: 1–17.*

AC

# Switch on here

*For in him you have been enriched in every way… you do not lack any spiritual gift… He will keep you strong to the end.*

Remember the TV series MASH, based on an American army medical unit during the Korean war? Supplies would be air-lifted in and dropped, for the medical unit to rush out and collect.

The supplies held everything vital for the continued health of the unit, and were seized upon at once. They were not piled up high in a corner, but unpacked with speed and gratitude. Paul reminds the Corinthians that they are in a spiritual warfare, but that their Divine Commander has made sure they have provisions so that they can not only survive to fight on, but flourish.

But for the air-lifted supplies to do any good, they had to be unpacked and used. The Corinthian Christians had not unpacked all the riches that God had given them, and so were in a mess. Does this remind you of your local church? Do you listen to wonderful liturgy and sermons, and wonder what this possibly has to do with the reality around you?

Well, but for the first nine verses of 1 Corinthians, the rest of Paul's letter—about growing into radiant faith, unquenchable hope, and fervent love—would be only a pious dream. Where would the power come from to transform these Corinthians? Paul does not despair, because he knows that the Corinthians have the power already, they just need to plug into it. God has not failed them; he is not far away.

It is the same with your church. Despite any problems, Jesus will sustain you too. 'God, who has called you into fellowship with his Son Jesus Christ… is faithful.'

And just as God will stick by our churches, it seems that we are to stick with them, too. Paul never told the more spiritual Corinthians to leave the carnal ones, and set up their own holy group.

No, they were in this together.

---

*Read Ephesians 1:3–14.*

                                    AC

# Let's not party

*There are quarrels among you… one of you says, 'I follow Paul',*
*another 'I follow Apollos', another 'I follow Cephas', still another*
*'I follow Christ'.*

If your church, or the Christian circles that you move in, has been blessed with any outstanding leaders, there is the downside—the danger of their success.

It is a great temptation for some Christians who have been genuinely helped by a particular Christian leader to begin to identify their Christian faith with that person. What he/she says 'goes'. The leader's emphasis on certain truths in the Christian message that are particularly relevant to that person now becomes the whole story, and other aspects of truth can get left out, forgotten.

The Corinthian church had allowed such emphases to develop into quarrelsome cliques. Paul heard of this, and was horrified. This was not at all how true Christian leadership should be seen.

Paul lists the various 'parties': the Paul party, the Apollos party, the Cephas (Peter) party, the Christ (?!) party. They were all outstanding leaders, men of God. Nowhere does Paul condemn them for the personality cults that have arisen around their names. It is the immaturity of the Corinthian Christians that was to blame.

It is worth a closer look at what Bible scholars believe these various groupings stood for, because they can still be found in local churches today. (We'll look at Paul today and the other three parties in tomorrow's reading.)

**The Paul party:** Many Corinthian Christians were deeply attached to Paul—he had brought them out of paganism to Christ. But it was a case of loving not wisely, but too well. For Paul had been gone for nearly two years now, and other leaders had arrived, sent by God, with work of their own to do. But the Paul-party rejected them out of hand.

There is probably no minister anywhere who has not arrived at a new church to discover a Paul party somewhere in the congregation. They are blind to what God has for them now, they want only the 'good old days' under Pastor so-and-so.

*Read 1 Thessalonians 5:12–13.*
**AC**

# Leave the party

*There are quarrels among you... one of you says, 'I follow Paul', another 'I follow Apollos', another 'I follow Cephas', still another 'I follow Christ'.*

**The Apollos party:** Apollos was from Alexandria (Acts 18.24–19.7), the Oxford or Cambridge of the day. He seems to have been a first-century C.S. Lewis, combining great learning and intellectual ability with fervent dedication to Christ and skill in explaining the gospel to pagans. This was irresistible to the more intellectual Corinthians. He said things they desperately wished *they* could have thought of saying.

**The Peter party:** Many Jewish converts in Corinth found it hard to give up aspects of the Jewish law they had practised all their lives. Peter, we learn from Acts, had this problem as well—the temptation to return to legalism about food laws was very strong. So this party represented the deep longings of these Jewish converts for their own cultural roots.

**The Christ party:** These folk sat very lightly indeed to any form of human leadership. Rather than living as members of the body of Christ, they preferred a direct private hotline to God. They are still around today, and can be prone to a faint but discernible air of spiritual superiority. They often intimidate other Christians, leaving them feeling spiritually inadequate. (It is not easy to cope with a *continual* 'The Lord said to me...')

Such people do not find it easy to even discuss issues with other Christians. If God has told them something is true, who are you to hold a different opinion?

Members of the Christ party invariably feel their local church is not spiritual enough. So they hive off and join a new church... and another, and another.

But Paul nowhere tells anyone to leave their local church, no matter what a mess it is. It is still the body of Christ, and the members need each other—and a variety of Christian leaders with different gifts.

---

*Read 1 Corinthians 12:12–26.*

**AC**

# Looking in the wrong direction

*Jews demand miraculous signs and Greeks look for wisdom, but
we preach Christ crucified: a stumbling block to Jews and
foolishness to Gentiles.*

If you reject Christ, where do you look for God? The non-believers of Paul's day used two different approaches, as have many people throughout history.

Some look for mighty miracles—God's big footprints on earth, as it were. Others build intellectual towers to give them 'lift' in reaching God.

The Jews wanted action. Jehovah had staged spectacular 'special effects' to rescue them from Egypt, and they wanted more miracles. Not plagues of frogs, but a Messiah that was a cross between Arnold Schwarzenegger, the archangel Gabriel, and Mel Gibson. An avenging heavenly patriotic fury that would descend from on high, blast all the Romans, and give the Jews back their land.

The Greeks shuddered at such physical ideas. To them, God was a remote, impersonal spirit, to be reached, if at all, through abstract reasoning. The thought of God involved in people's grubby little lives was abhorrent.

So the challenge of presenting Christ as the Truth is not new. For it is not modern thought that makes him unintelligible to non-Christians, it is worldly thought. There has *never* been a time when worldly wisdom appreciated Christianity.

Worldly wisdom does not look heavenward. It does not want to bow the knee and acknowledge a Creator. It shies away into endless eloquence and fine arguments over the meaning of life. Paul warns against wasting time in these discussions, because ultimately they go nowhere.

So how to connect with non-Christians? We can't—not on our own. We can only proclaim Christ crucified, testify to his living presence in our lives, and ask the Holy Spirit to open people's spiritual eyes.

Have you ever heard Billy Graham preach? Children understand every word. There is nothing subtle or elaborate. But his sermons have changed millions of lives: because they are charged with the electrifying power of the Holy Spirit.

---

*Read 2 Peter 1:3–11.*

AC

# Different rules apply

*Not many of you were wise… not many were influential; not many were of noble birth. But God chose the foolish things… the weak things… the lowly things… and the despised things… so that no one may boast before him.*

We need various qualifications to get anywhere in life. They're the basis on which people judge us, accept us or reject us. Paul here begins by listing the qualifications that opened doors for people in the first century, and which do so today.

**Wisdom:** academic success opens career doors. **Influence:** makes things happen. **Noble birth:** social connections put one a step ahead.

Of course, not all of us can muster such qualifications. And so we are squeezed out of those areas of life by people who *can* play the part. Too much 'squeezing out', and no room to move anywhere, can finally make us feel outcast. Our self-confidence is smashed, we feel inadequate, worthless.

But Paul is saying here that whatever measuring stick the world uses to judge us by, we must never fear that God uses the same criteria on us. In fact, quite the opposite.

God does not favour well-bred, articulate, brilliant, powerful and wealthy people. Their earthly power does not impress him. He is looking for people who recognize their desperate spiritual need, and who will respond to him in love.

When your hands are empty, you know you have nothing. This is why early Christianity spread among the lower classes more rapidly than among the cream of first-century Mediterranean society—the class-conscious Greeks and Romans. The lowly and destitute had no exalted illusions about their worth, and were in a position to receive. Their hands and hearts were open. God could do something with these people.

There is only one person to whom God gives special position and honour: his son, Jesus. So to qualify for God's favour, all we need do is to humble ourselves before the crucified Saviour.

And actually, if we want truly abundant life, with real wisdom, influence and spiritual power, Jesus is all we need.

---

*Read Luke 6:20–26.*

AC

# Heaven's lightning conductor

*I resolved to know nothing while I was with you except Jesus Christ and him crucified. I came to you in weakness and fear... my message and my preaching were not with wise and persuasive words, but with a demonstration of the Spirit's power.*

Here is a passage for anyone who testifies to their Christian faith, and especially for anyone who preaches. There are several things to notice about it.

First of all, the human side of things. Paul was thinking back to his own arrival in Corinth. Such was the reputation of the city that it had frightened even him. As a teenager I worked with YWAM for a time in the slums of Edinburgh, and I was scared stiff. It cheered me up to think that even the great apostle Paul had known fear.

Second, our fear and lack of fine rhetoric need not affect the success of our mission. Because we are not promoting a mere man-made intellectual position. The grand thing about evangelism is that we have a divinely given message. Our duty is simply to be faithful and tell it as it is.

Third, where is the power to do this? Again, this is given to us. The Holy Spirit shines through in this passage. Note the close relationship of the cross and the Holy Spirit. God's wisdom has been revealed in Jesus Christ, and the cross almost acts as a lightning conductor for the Holy Spirit. Wherever we lift up the cross before people, the Holy Spirit can flow down it with great power.

No wonder Paul made a conscious decision to abandon any natural wisdom. He wanted to concentrate on preaching Jesus Christ, and him crucified, so that the Spirit could demonstrate his power.

Such power ensured that the Corinthians met God for themselves. Then their faith would rest secure—not in the wisdom of men, but in the power of God.

Does our testifying hold up Christ, and bring down the power of the Spirit? If so, people's lives will be touched.

---

*Read John 15:26–27 and Acts 1:4–8.*

**AC**

# Would suit mature person...

*Yet among the mature we do impart wisdom. But we impart a secret and hidden wisdom of God... No eye has seen, nor ear heard, nor the heart of man conceived what God has prepared for those who love him.*

Christians sometimes remind me of different breeds of dogs. There are the elkhounds, who tend to wander off from God, distracted by their own noses. There are the terriers, who are happiest when fighting something, with or without their owner's permission. There are the springer spaniels, who are happiest at charismatic meetings, when they can joyously leap about with all four paws in the air.

Then there are the border collies, who have one fixed goal —to become as one with their master as possible. They rarely take their eyes from his face. Have you ever seen Crufts Dog Show on TV, when the border collies perform a Torvill and Dean dance routine with their owners, or obey a series of complicated instructions? Their empathy with their owners, and desire to please them, is legendary.

Paul was a border collie of a Christian. Elsewhere he wrote that 'for me to live is Christ, and to die is gain' (Philippians 1:21). He lived only to please and be near his Master.

This is Christian maturity, and it grows in us when we are receptive to the changes the Holy Spirit wants to make in our lives. Length of years is not a good guide: some Christians 'walk to heel' with Jesus, and so learn—and so grow—more in a year than others do in forty years. A heedless Irish setter of a Christian who barely recognizes his own name is not going to learn flyball in a hurry.

But the rewards of Christian maturity are spelt out in this passage. If we respond to God's training, we can become members of his family—loved, treasured and given great privileges. God has more treats in store for us than we can imagine—we just have to be willing to respond, and come when called.

---

*Read Philippians 3:12–21.*

AC

# Tune in

*We have not received the spirit of the world but the Spirit who is from God, that we may understand what God has freely given us.*

We are like radio receivers: we can pick up transmitted messages only if we are set on the same wavelength. If you doubt this, watch the way a conversation will develop at a party as different subjects come up. Mention football, and immediately many of the men present will light up. Mention classical music, book clubs, gardening, travel, and each time any aficionados of the subject will suddenly come to life. You are speaking their language, you are on their wavelength.

It is the same with Christians. When we are converted, we have a new radio wave band installed in us, and now we can pick up spiritual messages that go right by other, unconverted people. Most of us Christians have had the experience of meeting another Christian for the first time, and immediately establishing a rapport on a more intimate plane than we have been able to have with our non-Christian friends of many years. We share the same Spirit.

The Holy Spirit enables us to tune into each other, and most importantly, to tune into God. Without his help, we would have no spiritual discernment; it would all be gobbledegook.

Every Christian has the Holy Spirit within them, which is why Paul was so frustrated with the carnality of Christians at Corinth. Through the Holy Spirit, they had access to the very mind of Christ—but they were not making use of it.

Paul warns elsewhere that Christians who don't make use of the Holy Spirit can revert to behaving like unbelievers. The tragedy at Corinth, and in many churches today, is that people who are born again of the Spirit of God do not continue growing with him. They are almost stillborn spiritually.

---

*Read Ephesians 3:14—4:16.*
                                                        **AC**

# Stop fighting and grow up!

*Brothers, I could not address you as spiritual, but as worldly, mere infants in Christ… For since there is jealousy and quarrelling among you, are you not worldly?*

The Corinthian church had a major problem which affected its spiritual growth. It had a wrong view of Christian leadership. The Corinthian Christians were far too ready to put the spotlight on individuals, and to play one off against the other.

Instead of appreciating the different contributions that God had sent their way through the various Christian leaders who had visited them, they allied themselves to the memory of one leader only, and attacked the rest.

They thought 'either/or', not 'both/and'.

Such behaviour, Paul says bluntly, is puerile. Stop behaving like children in the playground who scream 'I'm going to play with you, but not you.' Have the sense to see that all of you are members of the body of Christ, and you have no business splitting into spiteful little cliques. You are to serve each other in love, not score points off each other.

In this case, the fault did not lie with the leaders, each of whom had served the Corinthian church with love and integrity. The fault lay in the Corinthians' spiritual immaturity.

Paul calls them brethren, because they have been baptized into Christ's body, but that is about as far as they have got. Baptized, but still on spiritual milk. Barely crawling, never mind walking in the Spirit.

What about your local church? Factions can arise for all sorts of reasons, and cause such heartache and tensions. Quarrels can bring the life of a local church to a spiritual standstill. They can break ministers' hearts, and destroy their ministry.

If you have such a church, do spend time praying for it. Somebody in there somewhere needs to grow up spiritually. Pray for your leaders, whom God has sent to you.

---

*Read 1 John 4:7–21 and Colossians 3:12–16.*

AC

# Gardening jobs

*What then is Apollos? What is Paul? Servants through whom you came to believe, as the Lord assigned to each. I planted, Apollos watered, but God gave the growth.*

Here's a knock on the head for any personality cult—not even 'who', but '*what*'? Paul's disdain is evident. We—Apollos and Paul—are *servants*, he says. We wait at table to serve you; we wait on the Lord for our responsibilities with regard to you.

Paul uses a vivid gardening metaphor to hammer his message home. The Corinthian church may have been planted by him, but it was watered by Apollos. Without Paul there would have been nothing. Without Apollos, what had begun would have died. Both gardening jobs are vital and inter-dependent. And both are totally dependent on God. It is God who gives the growth—the servants just prepare the conditions where growth can occur.

Paul here sketches a picture of what true Christian leadership in God's church should look like. There should be no lording it over others, as happens in the world. Instead, authority in the church, truly Christian authority, comes from those who lay down their lives for their brethren in service and availability.

Yet Paul does not denigrate the contribution that Apollos and he have made. Indeed, he calls them 'fellow workers with God'. Each Christian has distinctive, important work to do, which requires strenuous toil. Each contribution to God's work is essential.

And 'each will be rewarded according to his own labour'.

This has implications for you. You may know the job that God has assigned you in your local church—whatever skill or help you have to offer. It may be rewarding, and you may see growth—or you may be utterly frustrated, hampered by someone else who is not pulling his or her weight, and causing damage. Paul reassures you that God will honour whatever labour you put into his garden—he knows your efforts, even though the plants are stunted because of others' neglect.

---

*Read Colossians 3:23–25.*

AC

# Build it well

*For we are God's fellow-workers; you are God's fields, God's building.*

Our work as Christians with regard to other Christians will be judged one day. Was it of any real worth? Or was it all image, and no substance? Paul, who seems to like metaphors, now uses an architectural picture to explain this truth.

The Corinthian church, he says, is like God's building. He, Paul, was their skilled master builder. He laid the foundation stone. Some Corinthians wanted to think of Paul as the foundation stone, but Paul firmly denied this. The foundation stone is Jesus Christ... 'and someone else is building on it'. It is these builders of the church that come after, and their fate, that Paul wants to consider now.

Builders are given freedom by God to choose their materials. Some will use quality materials —gold, silver, costly stone—and some will use shoddy wood or straw. All of it may look great as it goes up—colourful, eye-catching.

But will it last? Paul warns of the day when fire will test the fundamental quality of the work each one of us has done. It doesn't matter how showy, attractive and popular the contribution was at the time—what was it really made of? Was it of God, through the Holy Spirit? Or was it something men built in the name of the church, but for their own benefit and glory?

Whatever survives the test will be rewarded.

No doubt every Christian's building efforts will have some straw mixed in with the gold. But sadly some of us will have the grief of seeing most of our lives' work burned up.

But Paul hastens to offer what reassurance he can: even bad building cannot tear them from the love of God. Smoking straw will not condemn them to eternal destruction. But all the same, their loss will be great, and they will enter the kingdom of heaven poorer for it.

Paul's message is, take care how you build. It is God's temple you are working on.

---

*Read Ephesians 4:1–16.*

**AC**

# Enjoy yourselves

*All things are yours, whether Paul or Apollos or Cephas or the world or life or death or the present or the future—all are yours, and you are of Christ, and Christ is of God.*

You can just imagine Paul getting really excited at this point and waving his arms about. He is saying, 'You are unimaginably rich! God has blessed you greatly—from the various Christian leaders he sends you, to your daily life in this beautifully created world. Beyond this world, after death, he will shower good things upon you. You will enjoy eternal life in the presence of a loving God, with blessings that we cannot here begin to imagine.'

Why? Because through the Holy Spirit, you are of Christ, and Christ is of God.

C.S. Lewis called God the great hedonist. It was he who created beauty and pleasure and he created them for our enjoyment. Some of the greatest Christian writers of the ages have written on this theme. We will close our present look at 1 Corinthians with quotations taken from their writings.

- God finds pleasure in us when we find pleasure in him. (*Augustine*)
- The more of heaven we cherish, the less of earth we covet. (*Anon.*)
- Joy is the serious business of heaven. (*C.S. Lewis*)
- The Christian ought to be a living doxology. (*Martin Luther*)
- If you have no joy in your religion, there's a leak in your Christianity somewhere. (*Billy Sunday*)
- Joy is the flag that is flown from the citadel of the heart when the King is in residence. (*Anon.*)
- God cannot give us happiness and peace apart from himself, because it is not there. There is no such thing. (*C.S. Lewis*)
- If you're not allowed to laugh in heaven, I don't want to go there. (*Martin Luther*)

*Read 1 Thessalonians 5:12–24.*
                                        AC

134

# DAY BY DAY WITH GOD

## MAGAZINE SECTION

# People of God

## Margaret Killingray

In our fast-changing world, Christians need to rethink how to respond to current moral and ethical issues.

The apostle Peter wrote a letter to the small groups of Christians scattered in the towns of Asia Minor in the first century AD, 2000 years ago. Their situation was hostile in many ways. They attempted to live the Christian way and were misunderstood and falsely accused of various anti-social activities. There were wives with non-Christian husbands, slaves with non-Christian masters, their neighbours were pagans and the local authorities were suspicious of the Christians.

Peter tells them to build up their Christian community so that they can encourage and support each other. He tells them to love each other intensely from the heart, and to remember that they are the people of God, chosen, loved, forgiven, with a joy and a hope that nothing can destroy, not even ill-treatment and persecution.

### Imitate Jesus

The main thrust of what Peter says is that they should imitate Jesus, particularly imitating the way he behaved when he was on trial before his execution. Peter is reminding the wives, slaves and other Christians in those small churches, that they could do very little about the unjust situations they were caught up in. They could not influence how their neightbours and local authorities treated them. Slaves with unjust masters had no rights, no way to get out of slavery. He tells them to do good even though they may be misunderstood and falsely accused of wrongdoing. He tells them to live good lives that can be seen, and not to talk back or argue. He tells them to restrain their tongues, to be peacemakers, not to return evil for evil, echoing the words of Jesus.

The emphasis in this letter is on endurance, on being humble and self-effacing, on being a loving and supportive community which helps its members to take the injustices and ill-treatment of the world, and does not return evil for evil—does not retaliate.

We sometimes need to be reminded that aggressiveness, fighting for one's rights, making sure that others know they are wrong, are not the best ways to be moral and good. But Peter's world was very different from ours. It was not a democracy, many people, including wives and slaves, had few rights, and endurance was the only option open to them. Today we do have the means to fight injustice. We are called to build up those who are oppressed so that they can seek redress. We can seek ways to end injustice and exploitation.

However, Christian communities are still called to build loving and supportive relationships that help us all as individuals to live the good life. In addition we are called singly and together to bring the reign of God into every part of the world around us, by getting involved in what is going on in our societies. We need to use our influence in ways that were not possible for most of those early Christians.

## Be involved

We need to be involved in questions of social welfare, homelessness and low pay; of medical ethics, euthanasia, abortion and fertility treatment; scientific and technological advance; in economic questions about world trade and third world debt; in environmental questions about the use of resources and the destruction of the natural world; in business ethics; in human rights, refugees and the role of the United Nations. All these are legitimate moral and ethical concerns for the Christian Church. But how on earth do we manage to do all that?

It is possible if we work together. In our Christian communities there will be those who can take on as their special responsibility the role of resource person who has the information and helps us all, when it becomes important, to think and act on the issues. We may need to take action, perhaps in small groups at local and national level. We may be called to join organisations and pressure groups and to bring their concerns to the church for prayer and information.

In a fast-changing world, Christians frequently have to rethink how they should respond to day-to-day issues. We need to train ourselves to have a Christian mind that can distinguish between the rules and attitudes that come from our fallen world, and those that come from God, even though they may often overlap. We need to know our Bibles so that our minds already have a Christian shape to their thinking. Above all, we need to escape from our isolation as individuals and be humble enough to pray and think together with other Christians.

Margaret Killingray's book *Choices* is published by BRF and is available from your local Christian bookshop or by using the order form on page 157.

# Temptations or testings?

*Beryl Adamsbaum*

Trials that come into our lives can be looked upon as temptations from the devil or as testings from God. We often tend to over-simplify as we categorically state that anything 'bad' is 'of the devil' and anything 'good' is 'of God'. But can't 'bad' things be used by God for our ultimate good? Sometimes we are genuinely perplexed as we wonder whether difficulties that come our way originate from our heavenly Father or from the one who is known as 'the father of lies'.

A look at scripture, however, shows us the glorious fact that God can transform any situation and bring good out of evil. Temptation is destructive, testing is constructive. The very things that the devil would use to destroy us are used by God to build us up, strengthen us and equip us. God is sovereign. We know that 'by his death [Jesus destroyed] him who holds the power of death—that is, the devil' (Hebrews 2:14). And we share in his victory!

Let us glance at some specific examples in scripture, beginning with the example of the Lord himself, who 'was led *by the Spirit*' into the desert 'to be tempted *by the devil*' (Matthew 4:1). Strange as it may seem to us, 'although he was a son, he learned obedience from what he suffered' (Hebrews 5:8). And if that was the case for Jesus, how much more for us! Luke tells us that 'when the devil had finished all this tempting, he left him... Jesus returned to Galilee *in the power of the Spirit*' (Luke 4:13–14).

## Power of the Spirit

I would venture to say that we cannot know the power of the Spirit in our lives unless we have been through trials and testings. Jesus was never in any doubt about the purpose for which he had come to this earth. 'My food,' he said, 'is to do the will of him who sent me' (John 4:34). In order to accomplish this, he needed the power of the Spirit. Are we here for any lesser purpose? If our 'food' is also to do the will of God, then surely we too need the power of the Holy Spirit in our lives. But the power of the Holy Spirit is not given to us for any personal gain or glorification, rather that God may be glorified.

The apostle Paul wrote, 'To keep me from being conceited… there was given me a thorn in the flesh, a messenger of Satan, to torment me' (2 Corinthians 12:7). Who gave him this 'thorn'? He refers to it as a 'messenger of Satan' sent to torment him. Satan's purposes, as we have already seen, are always destructive. And yet, Paul gives us a positive reason too for this 'thorn in the flesh'. It was to prevent him from becoming conceited. This is a good, constructive purpose, originating surely in God. We can only conclude then that God and the devil are both at work, and that, as in the example in the life of Jesus, that which Satan purposed for evil, God turned around and transformed into good. God's answer to Paul's repeated prayer for deliverance was, quite simply, 'My grace is sufficient for you, for my power is made perfect in weakness' (2 Corinthians 12:9).

If God's grace was sufficient for Paul, it is also sufficient for us today. His power is still 'made perfect in weakness'. Paul understood this perfectly, and it led him to utter that confident cry of victory and triumph: 'I will boast all the more gladly about my weaknesses, so that Christ's power may rest on me. That is why, for Christ's sake, I delight in weaknesses, in insults, in hardships, in persecutions, in difficulties. For when I am weak, then I am strong' (2 Corinthians 12:9–10). This same strength is available to us in our weakness. Can we echo these triumphant, victorious, confident, glorious words of the apostle Paul? Is this same experience ours? If not, it can be!

## Richly blessed

Having considered the examples of the Lord Jesus and the apostle Paul, we now turn to the Old Testament to look at a man who we are told was 'blameless and upright' (Job 1:1). A wealthy man, whom God had richly blessed, Job was known to be 'the greatest man among all the people of the East' (1:3). Wealth, riches, prestige, reputation—Job had everything going for him. He acknowledged, too, the source of his prosperity: 'He feared God and shunned evil.' And, we would like to add, he lived happily ever after.

But the book of Job gives us no account of a fairytale existence. Job was soon up against the harsh realities of life, facing extreme testings and trials. We can't help wondering why God actually brought him to Satan's notice! If God had not said to Satan, 'Have you considered my servant Job? There is no one on earth like him, he is blameless and upright, a man who fears God and shuns evil' (1:8), then none of the terrible tragedies recounted in this book would have fallen upon him. Job would have continued his easy, prosperous, God-fearing life. But would he, in the long run, have been better off? Didn't God have a reason for allowing Satan to test him? We know that God's purposes are always pure and just, resulting in our ultimate good and in his glory.

Satan's challenge is, of course, that it is not for nothing that Job fears God. 'Have you not put a hedge around him and his household and everything he has? You have blessed the work of his hands, so that his flocks and herds are spread throughout the land. But stretch out your hand and strike everything he has, and he will surely curse you to your face' (1:9–11). God takes up the challenge and tells Satan that 'everything he has is in your hands, but on the man himself do not lay a finger' (v. 12).

## God's sovereignty

Satan takes advantage of God's permission to test Job (but notice who sets the limits; notice who is really in control) and very soon Job finds himself bereft of children, servants, flocks and herds. All his wealth and possessions have gone. In his grief, he did an amazing thing: 'he fell to the ground in worship' (1:20). And we read that 'he did not sin by charging God with wrongdoing' (1:22). He was in no doubt of God's sovereignty: 'the Lord gave and the Lord has taken away' (1:21). True, the Lord did indeed give, but was it really the Lord who had taken away? Didn't we just read that this was the work of the devil? And he has not finished with his evil schemes, for back he comes before the Lord, who points out to him that 'Job still maintains his integrity' (2:3) in spite of the trouble that has come upon him. In spite of everything that happened to Job, he could still affirm with assurance, 'When he has tested me, I shall come forth as gold' (23:10). Again, there is no doubt in his mind that God is sovereign.

The apostle Peter picks up on this illustration of gold, explaining to his readers, 'Though now for a little while you may have had to suffer grief in all kinds of trials' these have come 'so that their faith—of greater worth than gold, which perishes even though refined by fire—may be proved genuine and may result in praise, glory and honour when Jesus Christ is revealed' (1 Peter 1:6–7).

The book of Job ends on a triumphant note, as the Lord leads him into a relationship of greater trust. 'The Lord blessed the latter part of Job's life more than the first' (42:12).

So there is a happy ending after all! If only we would learn to trust God in the darkest times and remember that 'in all things God works for the good of those who love him, who have been called according to his purpose' (Romans 8:28). We shall leave the final affirmation of faith to Job: 'Though he slay me, yet will I hope in him' (13:15).

# It's life, but not as we want it

*Diana Archer*

Why did only one man receive healing at the Pool of Bethesda? Why not some of the others? They were all there for the same reason, waiting for a chance of healing, so why did Jesus pick out just that one man?

Having thought myself into the crowds which gathered around Jesus, in order to write this edition's notes, I realized at the end that I still had some questions. I saw that the reactions people gave to Jesus were not dependent on him. He did not orchestrate them, and they were not under his control. Some people thought he was wonderful and followed him everywhere; others thought he was a dangerous fraud. Some dismissed him; others believed in him. I am sure that the same range of responses is still around today. I like to think that, had I been a first-century Jew, I would have been among those who were immediately fascinated by and responded willingly to Jesus. But would there have been days when I was confused as well as delighted by his actions? Certainly, there were occasions when Jesus healed everyone at one of his teach-ins (for example, Matthew 9:35). But there were also times, as at the pool, when he chose one or two for miraculous dealings and left the rest. He raised Jairus' daughter from the dead, Lazarus and the widow of Nain's son. Although I accept that, theologically, these actions demonstrated his authority over life and death, what about all the other people who lost daughters, sons and brothers while Jesus was around? What about compassion for them? If people came to him for healing, did Jesus ever look them in the eye and say, 'No'?

## Questions

I am asking these questions because it seems to me that this is the situation we are faced with today. Jesus does not always answer healing requests with a 'Yes'—not in the way we want it, anyway. We hear of remarkable millions-strong revival meetings in Africa where healings abound. We see advertisements for crusades in our towns and wonder whether to believe the miracle claims. We may even have ventured to a meeting or two and seen miracles for ourselves. But that still leaves the folk who did not receive the life-changing event they coveted.

Recently I sat with a childless couple and shared for a moment in their grief and frustration. Why, when Jesus could fix things, doesn't he? Yet when we came to pray with them, I sensed only God's love and compassion for them in their pain. I admired their struggle to come to terms creatively with a situation they did not choose. They never wanted life to be this way. Soon after that, I heard Canon John Gakwandi talk of the genocide in Rwanda in 1994. He spoke graphically of squashing himself and his family into sideboards while the killers rampaged through the streets, destroying everyone in their path. For three months, his family and others subsisted in a tiny compound, waiting for the horror to end. Rainwater and avocados saved them from starvation, while many of their friends and neighbours were butchered outside. Canon John gives the credit for his survival entirely to the grace of God. He now heads up Solace Ministries, a Christian organization responding to the continuing fallout from the bloodshed, giving essential emotional and practical support. For so many widows and orphans, life is absolutely not how they wanted it. I think of the Holocaust, the ethnic 'cleansing' of recent years in Europe, the Chernobyl meltdown. Each of these historical disasters come into real people's lives and affect them for ever.

## Significance

Less dramatically, but with huge significance to the individuals, there are other ways in which life does not work out how we want. Think of the single person who longs to be married, the married person locked into an unhappy union, the widowed, the fatherless, the unemployed, those who lose their health and yet have to live on with reduced capabilities.

Obviously the list is endless. I have yet to meet anyone who does not have to face the unwanted in their lives in one way or another. The unwanted brings frustration at our inability to make life smooth, and anger that it is rough at all. Something inside rages at the injustice of it all. Genocide is wrong. Poverty is wrong. Childlessness is wrong. It's life, but not as we want it.

We cannot, of course, go too far down the 'why-don't-you-fix-it-Jesus?' road. In every Gospel example of Jesus' interaction with human beings, the latter receive consistent compassion if they are in need. The only time when Jesus connects with suffering and does not alleviate it is when it is his own. And here we encounter his humanity, for this was, for Jesus, the situation he did not want. He begged, as we beg, for it to be changed. He did not want to face the unfaceable. But he had to go through with it, as we do. Perhaps the big difference is that, for us, we can choose to have the Father's companionship and understanding along the way. Jesus had to face his nightmares alone. 'My God, my God, why have you forsaken me?'

But if this was Jesus' hardest moment, he must truly understand ours too. We too are asked to accept the unacceptable. We have to come to terms with what should not have happened.

## Acceptance

How? I am still learning on this one. It seems to be something to do with relating to God in the middle of the pain and fury. Shutting him out gets nowhere. Is it about trusting God anyway, despite catastrophe? Easier said than done. Perhaps we need his help and that of others, to commit ourselves to the journey of acceptance. Often we need so much emotional healing, whether or not we receive the physical stuff. We need God's help to forgive people and events and even God himself. I honestly think that accepting the unacceptable is one of the most difficult things we are ever asked to do.

Yet I also see that managing to do so can bring amazing results. That is what happened with Jesus. This paradox nestles at the heart of the gospel: out of death, life. Out of the charred remains of disaster, new possibilities emerge. All of the unwanted, unacceptable, unfaceable situations of life can be transformed by power and grace. It may not ever be life as we want it, but our God specializes in bringing resurrection where we least expect it.

Diana Archer's book *Who'd Plant a Church?* is published by Christina Press and is available from your local Christian bookshop or by using the order form on page 156.

# Dear Paul... am I the only one?

## Bridget Plass writes...

What if it were possible to ask Paul all the questions we would like to ask and to challenge him on his more controversial statements. What might he have to say to us? I don't know how he would choose to reply if we wrote to him, but trying to guess has been great fun. I hope my guesses might prove helpful to those of you who have struggled to reconcile some of Paul's most famous declarations with some of his most dogmatic...

So allow me to invite you to join me in the company of this controversial man of God. Just how familiar are we with everything Paul wrote? How much do we know about the cultural context in which he operated? This book aims to catch a glimpse, not only of the passion that drove him on, but also of the compassion he had for those little churches that he founded and the individuals who were involved with them. Perhaps we will come to understand a little more why his 'dear friend the doctor' Luke liked and respected him so much, and why Timothy remained close to him throughout his ministry and appeared to love him dearly. We may even stop seeing him as a single-issue fanatic, and indeed start to question whether our obsession with the comparatively few remarks he made about women makes us just as intolerant as he seems to be.

You can find further details on page 154, and an order form on page 157. Alternatively, *Dear Paul... am I the only one?* is available from your local Christian bookshop.

# Tricia

**Dear Paul**

I am in the middle of the very worst week in my entire life. Nothing you can say or do will help me and my family, but I just want to talk to you so much. My darling, darling daughter has died, Paul. She has gone. I still can't take it in, but each morning I wake up feeling sick and strange, and then I remember. She died suddenly, you see. We didn't know she was even ill. She was so lovely, Paul, such a good, good girl. She was clever and kind and always lovely to her little brother. She never went through any nasty patches. Well, not really. We love—loved—her so much. What can you say to me, Paul? Where is she? Why has this happened to us? She didn't deserve to die.

She was seventeen, just going into the sixth form at school, her future ahead of her. She went to church most Sunday evenings and to youth group. I don't know if she had actually made the decision, if you know what I mean—I don't think she felt there was any urgency. She hasn't always found it easy to go along with everything the church said, but she was full of hope, determined that she and her friends would make a difference. And I know she prayed sometimes, especially for her friends.

How can this have been what God intended for her, Paul? Someone the other day asked me if I felt angry. I just feel devastated and very confused, especially with you!

You see, we've had loads of cards and one of them had some of your words in it. They churned me up a bit. It almost sounded as if you thought death was a good thing to happen. I know you can't have meant that, even allowing for the fact that you couldn't know how it feels to have a child die. But for a moment I hated you— hated your complacency, your matter-of-factness.

I don't feel that now. All I want is to know—well, you know what I want to know. Please help me. I feel utterly, utterly lost. Can you help me?

Yours,

**Tricia Bowland**

## Dear Tricia

May I first extend my deepest sympathy to you and your family. You are quite correct. There was nothing in my experience to equal your present tragedy.

Tricia, I am not at liberty to tell you what I know you want to hear more than anything in the world. What I can do is to tell you that you must ask for the faith to trust that, just as surely as Eutychus was brought back to life in this world, so will you daughter be in the next. She will stand before Christ's throne, and because of what he did for her two thousand years ago, she will stand holy, faultless and irreproachable. Tricia, I am going to try to explain to you what I meant when I said that 'for me to live is Christ, to die is gain'. I wasn't saying that death is enjoyable. Neither was I being morbid. What I was trying to say was that, in a very real sense, when we accept the Lord Jesus into our lives we experience the only death that really counts—the death of death. From that moment, our lives become hidden in Christ. He is our life and we can never die in any sense that matters. It is just a matter of time before we are allowed to go home, and in the meantime we have to get on with living in our bodies here. We try to make it our goal to please him, but while we are on earth we will never be able to fulfil the longing we experience to actually be with him. I make this sound very matter-of-fact, but it was a passion which burned in me. The more I got to know him, the more I yearned to be with him. After all, all the apostles except me had actually known him while he was here on earth. I lived impatiently with the truth that I simply had to wait until I was allowed to go home to live my life in his presence. So, in other words, while I knew that I had Christ in me in this life, only death would allow me to have what I wanted most in the world, to actually be with him. It was therefore a very personal desire that I expressed when I was writing to my dear friends in Philippi.

Dearest Tricia, it is my deepest wish for you to understand that although it is quite awful for you no longer to have your wonderful daughter, it is not death that has taken her from you. Death has no power over her. When our Lord and Saviour died on the cross, he didn't do so in order to conquer Rome, although, in my ignorance, I had believed that Rome was the enemy our Messiah would deal with. No, indeed, our Lord was after a far more dangerous adversary, namely death itself. At the moment Christ died, death lost its sting completely. The last enemy had been destroyed, swallowed up in victory; and nothing could separate God's children from him ever again.

So Tricia, she has simply gone home before you. Her house was ready before yours. Having served him in her short life, she can now enjoy him for ever more. She can never be hurt. She can never die. But, of course, you cannot fully understand this. Your tears tell the truth. You have lost your most precious jewel and for a time nothing will even begin to explain it to you or enable you to rejoice in her blessings. All I can promise you, my dear friend, is that as long as we are on earth we can only ever expect to catch an occasional glimpse of the truth. I used a very simple illustration all those years ago which I believe will still have the same relevance to you. I said that while we are on earth it is as if we can only see a very poor reflection of something which we know by faith is the truth himself. It is frustratingly hazy and blurred. Only when we have passed through the gate which we still call death, but which we should call life, will we see him face to face and be able to know him as clearly as he knows us.

In the meantime, I know that this same risen Lord, Jesus himself, so aptly described by Isaiah as being 'a man of sorrows and familiar with suffering' will want to be there for you in your agony, and I know he will be willing to receive all you need to say, so talk to him.

Your friend,

*Paul*

## Dear Paul

I am sorry to pester you again so soon, but something has happened which has upset me even more, and I don't know who else to turn to. My son James was picking up the post from our front mat. There was a copy of the church magazine with a special insert saying when the funeral is to be, and some bills, but almost all of it was letters and cards expressing their sympathy and saying something lovely about our beautiful girl. And there was something else. There was a note in an unmarked envelope which simply said 'THE WAGES OF SIN IS DEATH'. I found James all screwed up in an armchair, shouting and screaming in his shock and grief, this horrible bit of paper in his hand. I know there are and have always been sick people around, but it's got inside my head and I can't get it out of my thoughts. Lucy had some rather odd schoolfriends and she had recently taken to wearing those awful clunky shoes and loads of black, and she had even had an eyebrow pierced. She wasn't like some of her friends who used to go out for an evening looking as though they were going trick-or-treating, if you know what that means, with loads of black lipstick and dark smudgy eyes. But she'd had this ink tattoo done on her ankle and she did look a bit different from most of her church friends. Her granny and I used to laugh about it. We knew she hadn't really changed, but I know some of the older folk in the church had problems with the way she looked.

Paul, tell me it can't be true. Tell me this illness which has taken her away isn't her fault. I don't really believe it can be so, or that God could be so cruel or so lacking in insight, but...

I tried to take in what you said in your letter but it was hard, you know. Now this.

Yours,

**Tricia**

*Dear Tricia,*
I am deeply sorry to hear what has happened to you and to your family. Now, I have two things to say to you and I want you to listen carefully because you are in danger. You are very vulnerable at the moment. It is essential that you keep your eyes firmly on the one who loves you and see to it that no one takes you captive through the hollow and deceptive philosophy which depends on human tradition and the basic principles of this world rather than on Christ.

First, you say that Lucy had a tattoo on her ankle. Did you know she had another stamp on her? Not easily visible, and definitely not removable with soap and water. At the moment she accepted Jesus as her Lord, she received a spiritual birthmark. She was stamped with the seal of the Holy Spirit of the promise who is the pledge of our inheritance. That is what her Father in heaven saw when he looked at her. You say she dressed slightly outrageously. The young have always wanted to make their mark, always wanted to outdo their elders in their passion and their zeal. She was no exception. What made her exceptional was that she seemed to have found a way to be all things to all people without compromising herself. She prayed for her friends. She knew them well enough to realize that they were not yet ready to see what she had as something they needed, and she loved them well enough to realize that prayer was the only way she could hope to ensure their future freedom.

Now, I think that's enough said on that subject, don't you?

Let us now look at the content of the note. First of all, and without trying to justify myself, I want to quote the whole sentence as I wrote it. What I actually said was, 'The wages paid by sin is death; the gift freely given by God is eternal life in Christ Jesus our Lord.' I did not mean that if you die you must have sinned. Why would I have said that? Everyone sins and everyone dies, so it would have been rather a waste of paper, wouldn't it? Don't forget, my letters were written on papyrus, which was costly and complicated to produce. The strips of bulrush pith of which our paper was constituted had to be imported from the banks of the Nile, so I'd hardly waste it on saying silly, obvious things of no worth. No, what I meant was that the evil one is the ultimate deceiver. The wage he has in store for his servants is spiritual death. Try to remember what I said to you in my last letter. For God's children, death is simply the door though which they run into his presence. For the slaves captured during their lifetime by the evil one, death is the door to a life without Christ. You say your daughter was full of hope—hope for the future. You too can have hope, hope in a God who does not lie and who gave his promise before time began that life in Christ is eternal. Wear this hope as your helmet to protect you from the arrows of doubt with which the evil one will try to pierce your thoughts.

Lastly, I want to refer briefly to the writer of the letter. I want you to pray for her because she is in even greater danger than you. I fear that, despite her involvement in your church, she is in fact a servant of sin, feeling no obligation to uprightness and having the desire to dominate and degrade. May your faith depend not on human wisdom, but on the power of God. Always remember, dear Tricia, that God at his most foolish is wiser than the cleverest person, and at his weakest is stronger than human beings at their strongest.

Yours with love and concern for you all,

## Paul

Dear Paul... am I the only one? is published by BRF and is available from your local Christian bookshop or by using the order form on page 157.

# Other Christina Press titles

**Who'd Plant a Church?** Diana Archer
£5.99 in UK
Planting an Anglican church from scratch, with a team of four—
two adults and two children—is an unusual adventure even in
these days. Diana Archer is a vicar's wife who gives a distinctive
perspective on parish life.

**Pathway Through Grief** edited by Jean Watson
£6.99 in UK
Ten Christians, each bereaved, share their experience of loss.
Frank and sensitive accounts offering comfort and reassurance
to those recently bereaved. Jean Watson has lost her own husband and believes that those involved in counselling will also
gain new insights from these honest personal chronicles.

**God's Catalyst** Rosemary Green
£8.99 in UK
Rosemary Green's international counselling ministry has prayer
and listening to God at its heart. Changed lives and rekindled
faith testify to God's healing power. Here she provides insight,
inspiration and advice for both counsellors and concerned
Christians who long to be channels of God's Spirit to help those
in need. *God's Catalyst* is a unique tool for the non-specialist
counsellor; for the pastor who has no training; for the Christian
who wants to come alongside hurting friends.

**Angels Keep Watch** Carol Hathorne
£5.99 in UK
A true adventure showing how God still directs our lives, not
with wind, earthquake or fire, but by the still, small voice.
    'Go to Africa.' The Lord had been saying it for over fory years.
At last, Carol Hathorne had obeyed, going out to Kenya with her
husband. On the eastern side of Nairobi, where tourists never
go, they came face to face with dangers, hardships and poverty
on a daily basis, but experienced the joy of learning that
Christianity is still growing in God's world.

### Not a Super-Saint  Liz Hansford
£6.99 in UK

'You might have thought Adrian Plass… had cornered the market in amusing diary writing. Well, check out Liz Hansford's often hilarious account of life as a Baptist minister's wife in Belfast. Highly recommended.' *The New Christian Herald*

Liz Hansford describes the outlandish situations which arise in the Manse, where life is both fraught and tremendous fun. *Not a Super-Saint* is for the ordinary Christian who feels they must be the only one who hasn't quite got it all together.

### The Addiction of a Busy Life  Edward England
£5.99 in UK

Twelve lessons from a devastating heart attack. Edward, a giant of Christian publishing in the UK, and founder of Christina Press, shares what the Lord taught him when his life nearly came to an abrupt end. Although not strictly a Christina title (Edward lacks the gender qualifications), we believe you may want to buy this for the busy men in your lives.

'A wonderful story of success and frailty, of love and suffering, of despair and hope. If you are too busy to read this book, you are too busy.' *Dr Michael Green*

### Life Path  Luci Shaw
£5.99 in UK

Personal and spiritual growth through journal writing. Life has a way of slipping out of the back door while we're not looking. Keeping a journal can enrich life as we live it, and bring it all back later. Luci Shaw shows how a journal can also help us grow in our walk with God.

### Precious to God  Sarah Bowen
£5.99 in UK

Two young people, delighted to be starting a family, have their expectations shattered by the arrival of a handicapped child. And yet this is only the first of many difficulties to be faced. What was initially a tragedy is, through faith, transformed into a story of inspiration, hope and spiritual enrichment.

All the above titles are available from Christian bookshops everywhere, or in case of difficulty, direct from Christina Press using the order form on page 156.

# Other BRF titles

*Dear Paul... am I the only one?*  Bridget Plass
*Readings for times of loss*
£5.99 in UK

In this book, Bridget Plass uses the concept of imagined corre-spondence between the apostle Paul and a widely varying group of contemporary men and women to explore the apostle's con-troversial teaching in a way that is at the same time informative, factual and fun.

In her role as a Christian speaker, Bridget has met many who have expressed their views of Paul to her. Her use of the two-way fictional correspondence allows her to explore the real and deep issues she has encountered against the biblical background of Acts and Paul's letters to the early Church.

The result is a book which is deeply insightful and designed to minister to the needs of all those who have struggled with the challenge of reconciling Paul's theology to their own lives, and perhaps have experienced self-doubt as a result.

*A Time to Wait*  Liz Morris
*Bible insights on trusting God's timing*
£5.99 in UK

In today's 'instant access' culture, the idea of waiting seems irrel-evant, outdated. People like fast cars, fast food, money at the touch of a button. Every part of life is caught up in the rush, with even Christians developing a taste for faith geared to quick answers, problem-solving, and miracles on demand.

So what happens when we find God asking us to wait?

This is a boook for everybody who is trying to live according to God's timing—perhaps reluctantly! It is for those who may fear that God has even forgotten them, despite the promises he gives through the Bible. Reflecting on some familiar Bible stories and characters, Liz Morris sets out some of the lessons that can help us along the way.

*'We are indebted to Liz for sharing her insights with such wisdom and love.'* (Faith Forster)

**Choices**  Margaret Killingray
*Deciding right and wrong today*
£5.99 in UK
'Should I give up my career to care for my mother?'

'Should I forgive my husband for a one night stand?'

'Should we build a new conservatory when people elsewhere are starving?'

How do we go about making decisions, especially in a so-called 'grey area' where no choice seems ideal? How can the Bible really help us in choosing between right and wrong? *Choices* explores the influences that shape our thinking and the difficulty of making moral decisions in the real world, especially for Christians who have to learn to negotiate the tensions between their own feelings and weaknesses, the pressures of today's culture and God's law of love.

*'Full of practical wisdom for making the most of life.'* (Rob Warner)

(This book was previously advertised as *Taking Hold of Life*.)

*2 Corinthians (PBC)*  Aída Besançon Spencer
£7.99 in UK
Paul's second letter to the young church at Corinth is forged in the heat of difficult circumstances. False teachers were challenging the apostle's authority and he also had to present a defence of the practice of church discipline for those who had in some way strayed. Throughout this passionate letter, despite the believers' failings, their lack of commitment and their criticism of his ministry, Paul's love and concern for them shine through.

*2 Corinthians* is just one title in BRF's *The People's Bible Commentary* series. Planned to cover the whole Bible, the series takes a daily readings approach that brings together both personal devotion and reflective study. Combining the latest scholarship with straightforward language and a reverent attitude to Scripture, it aims to instruct the head and warm the heart. The authors come from around the world and across the Christian traditions, and offer serious yet accessible commentary.

All the above titles are available from Christian bookshops everywhere or, in case of difficulty, direct from BRF using the order form on page 157.

# Christina Press Publications Order Form

All of these publications are available from Christian bookshops everywhere or, in case of difficulty, direct from the publisher. Please make your selection below, complete the payment details and send your order with payment as appropriate to:

**Christina Press Ltd, 17 Church Road, Tunbridge Wells, Kent TN1 1LG**

|      |                          | Qty | Price | Total |
|------|--------------------------|-----|-------|-------|
| 8700 | God's Catalyst           | ____ | £8.99 | ____ |
| 8702 | Precious to God          | ____ | £5.99 | ____ |
| 8703 | Angels Keep Watch        | ____ | £5.99 | ____ |
| 8704 | Life Path                | ____ | £5.99 | ____ |
| 8705 | Pathway Through Grief    | ____ | £6.99 | ____ |
| 8706 | Who'd Plant a Church?    | ____ | £5.99 | ____ |
| 8708 | Not a Super-Saint        | ____ | £6.99 | ____ |
| 8705 | The Addiction of a Busy Life | ____ | £5.99 | ____ |

| POSTAGE AND PACKING CHARGES | | | | |
|------|------|--------|----------|---------|
|      | UK   | Europe | Surface  | Air Mail |
| £7.00 & under | £1.25 | £2.25 | £2.25 | £3.50 |
| £7.10–£29.99 | £2.25 | £5.50 | £7.50 | £11.00 |
| £30.00 & over | free | prices on request | | |

Total cost of books £ _____
Postage and Packing £ _____
TOTAL £ _____

All prices are correct at time of going to press, are subject to the prevailing rate of VAT and may be subject to change without prior warning.

Name _____

Address _____

_____

_____Postcode _____

Total enclosed £ _____ (cheques should be made payable to 'Christina Press Ltd')

☐ Please send me further information about Christina Press publications

# BRF Publications Order Form

All of these publications are available from Christian bookshops everywhere, or in case of difficulty direct from the publisher. Please make your selection below, complete the payment details and send your order with payment as appropriate to:

**BRF, Peter's Way, Sandy Lane West, Oxford OX4 6HG**

| | | Qty | Price | Total |
|---|---|---|---|---|
| 038 3 | Dear Paul... am I the only one? | ____ | £5.99 | _____ |
| 048 0 | A Time to Wait | ____ | £5.99 | _____ |
| 194 0 | Choices | ____ | £5.99 | _____ |
| 073 1 | PBC: 2 Corinthians | ____ | £7.99 | _____ |

| POSTAGE AND PACKING CHARGES | | | | |
|---|---|---|---|---|
| | UK | Europe | Surface | Air Mail |
| £7.00 & under | £1.25 | £2.25 | £2.25 | £3.50 |
| £7.10–£29.99 | £2.25 | £5.50 | £7.50 | £11.00 |
| £30.00 & over | free | prices on request | | |

Total cost of books £ _____

Postage and Packing £ _____

TOTAL £ _____

All prices are correct at time of going to press, are subject to the prevailing rate of VAT and may be subject to change without prior warning.

Name _____

Address _____

_____

_____ Postcode _____

Total enclosed £ _____ (cheques should be made payable to 'BRF')

Payment by: cheque ❑ postal order ❑ Visa ❑ Mastercard ❑ Switch ❑

Card no. ☐☐☐☐ ☐☐☐☐ ☐☐☐☐ ☐☐☐☐

Card expiry date ☐☐☐☐   Issue number (Switch) ☐☐☐☐

Signature _____

(essential if paying by credit/Switch card)

❑ Please send me further information about BRF publications

**Visit the BRF website at www.brf.org.uk**

DBDWG0201                                    BRF is a Registered Charity

# Subscription Information

Each issue of *Day by Day with God* is available from Christian book-shops everywhere. Copies may also be available through your church Book Agent or from the person who distributes Bible reading notes in your church.

Alternatively you may obtain *Day by Day with God* on subscription direct from the publishers. There are two kinds of subscription:

Individual Subscriptions are for four copies or less, and include postage and packing. To order an annual Individual Subscription please complete the details on page 160 and send the coupon with payment to BRF in Oxford. You can also use the form to order a Gift Subscription for a friend.

Church Subscriptions are for five copies or more, sent to one address, and are supplied post free. Church Subscriptions run from 1 May to 30 April each year and are invoiced annually. To order a Church Subscription please complete the details opposite and send the coupon to BRF in Oxford. You will receive an invoice with the first issue of notes.

All subscription enquiries should be directed to:

**BRF**
**Peter's Way**
**Sandy Lane West**
**Oxford**
**OX4 6HG**

Tel: 01865 748227
Fax: 01865 773150
E-mail: subscriptions@brf.org.uk.

# Church Subscriptions

The Church Subscription rate for *Day by Day with God* will be £9.90 per person until April 2002.

☐ I would like to take out a church subscription for _____ (Qty) copies.

☐ Please start my order with the September 2001/January 2002/May 2002* issue. I would like to pay annually/receive an invoice with each edition of the notes*.
(*Please delete as appropriate)

Please do not send any money with your order. Send your order to BRF and we will send you an invoice. The Church Subscription year is from May to April. If you start subscribing in the middle of a subscription year we will invoice you for the remaining number of issues left in that year.

Name and address of the person organising the Church Subscription:

Name _____

Address _____

_____

Postcode _____Telephone_____
Church _____
Name of Minister _____

Name and address of the person paying the invoice if the invoice needs to be sent directly to them:

Name _____

Address _____

_____

Postcode _____Telephone_____

Please send your coupon to:

**BRF**
**Peter's Way**
**Sandy Lane West**
**Oxford**
**OX4 6HG**

DBDWG0201    The Bible Reading Fellowship is a Registered Charity

# Individual Subscriptions

☐ I would like to give a gift subscription (please complete both name and address sections below)

☐ I would like to take out a subscription myself (complete name and address details only once)

The completed coupon should be sent with appropriate payment to BRF. Alternatively, please write to us quoting your name, address, the subscription you would like for either yourself or a friend (with their name and address), the start date and credit card number, expiry date and signature if paying by credit card.

Gift subscription name _____

Gift subscription address _____

_____ Postcode _____

Please send to the above for one year, beginning with the September 2001/ January2002/May 2002 issue: (delete as applicable)

|  | UK | Surface | Air Mail |
|---|---|---|---|
| *Day by Day with God* | ☐ £11.55 | ☐ £12.90 | ☐ £15.15 |
| *2-year subscription* | ☐ £19.99 | N/A | N/A |

Please complete the payment details below and send your coupon, with appropriate payment, to The Bible Reading Fellowship, Peter's Way, Sandy Lane West, Oxford OX4 5HG.

Your name _____

Your address _____

_____ Postcode _____

Total enclosed £ _____ (cheques should be made payable to 'BRF')

Payment by: cheque ☐ postal order ☐ Visa ☐ Mastercard ☐ Switch ☐

Card no. ☐☐☐☐ ☐☐☐☐ ☐☐☐☐ ☐☐☐☐

Card expiry date ☐☐☐☐  Issue number (Switch) ☐☐☐☐

Signature _____

(essential if paying by credit/Switch card)

NB: These notes are also available from Christian bookshops everywhere.

DBDWG0201     The Bible Reading Fellowship is a Registered Charity